CE

THE WASHINGTON PAPERS
Volume VI

113 · 1 B · 171 ①

P. W. 144 lau

/eorer.

56: MEXICAN FOREIGN POLICY UNDER ECHEVERRÍA

Yoram Shapira

THE CENTER FOR STRATEGIC AND INTERNATIONAL STUDIES
Georgetown University, Washington, D.C.

SAGE PUBLICATIONS
Beverly Hills / London

For information address:

SAGE PUBLICATIONS, INC.   SAGE PUBLICATIONS LTD
275 South Beverly Drive 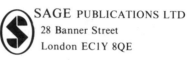 28 Banner Street
Beverly Hills, California 90212   London EC1Y 8QE

International Standard Book Number 0-8039-1096-7

Library of Congress Catalog Card No. 78-58423

FIRST PRINTING

---

*When citing a Washington Paper, please use the proper form. Remember to cite the
series title and include the paper number. One of the two following formats can be
adapted (depending on the style manual used):*

(1) HASSNER, P. (1973) "Europe in the Age of Negotiation." The Washington
Papers, I, 8. Beverly Hills and London: Sage Pubns.

OR

(2) Hassner, Pierre. 1973. *Europe in the Age of Negotiation.* The Washington Papers,
vol. 1, no. 8. Beverly Hills and London: Sage Publications.

CONTENTS

ACKNOWLEDGEMENTS

This study was prepared under the auspices of the Leonard Davis Institute for International Relations of the Hebrew University of Jerusalem. Special thanks are due to the institute's staff and its secretary, Sophie Amir, for their good will and constant help.

The author wishes to express his thanks to Ethel Goldman, Judy Ron, and Emanuel Adler, students of the Hebrew University of Jerusalem, for their valuable assistance and advice.

I. INTRODUCTION: LINKAGE POLITICS AND THE MEXICAN CASE

The development and promotion of a new Mexican foreign policy under the leadership of President Luis Echeverría (1970–1976) took place in the wake of a severe internal political crisis. Cumulative long-range socioeconomic pressures and political frustrations joined with short-range catalysts to produce a major national upheaval in 1968, just prior to Luis Echeverría's ascendance to the presidency of Mexico. The 1968 crisis was clearly of a domestic nature; it bore on such fundamental and interrelated issues as the distribution of resources and opportunities among socioeconomic strata, political alienation versus participation, and the very legitimacy of the manipulation of "revolutionary" ideology and democratic-participatory symbolism by a monopolistic power elite. Those who challenged the system in 1968 paid scant attention to foreign policy issues. Yet, the president who was to bear the brunt of this unprecedented domestic crisis and its aftermath is likely to be remembered in Mexican political annals primarily as a major innovator of his nation's foreign policy. This seeming contradiction makes greater sense once the interrelationship between Echeverría's domestic and foreign policies is established.

As has been noted by James N. Rosenau (1966: 33), foreign policies of modernizing societies are often shaped by internal needs, such as the need to sustain charismatic leadership, or to confer identity and prestige on the elite, or to divert attention from internal problems. Rosenau (1967: 25) has also observed that leaders of developing nations often seem better able to overcome domestic strife and inertia by focusing upon the hostility of the external environment than by stressing the need for internal measures. They thus attempt to solve domestic issues by redefining them as falling within the foreign policy area.

Even earlier, Robert C. Good made some observations

8

about the performance of leaders of developing states in the
international sphere that cast particular insight into Echeverría's behavior from 1970 to 1976. Good argued that these
leaders often turn to the international arena to validate their
capacity to act. Almost prophetically, he stated (1962: 9):

> Leader X appears before the United Nations. His speech is later
> featured at home as the occasion when X set the world aright, advising
> his fellow statesmen of the course that must be pursued to avoid ruin
> and achieve justice. For a leader of a new state, all the world — the
> UN, regional conferences, or state visits — is a stage on which to play
> a heroic role, partly for its impact on an audience back home.

Luis Echeverría undertook two broad types of foreign
policy decisions while president of Mexico which can be
viewed as innovative within the context of Mexico's traditional conduct of international affairs. These initiatives also
exemplify linkage politics because they depict a strong
relationship between domestic and foreign policy. One category is represented by narrow front initiatives, such as
Echeverría's Chilean and Spanish policies, the other by
comprehensive revisionist attempts, epitomized by Mexico's
Charter of States' Economic Rights and Duties, and later by
the proposal for a Third World economic system.

Both categories emerged while internal reform was proving
increasingly difficult to attain; the resultant frustrations
proved crucial in shifting Echeverría's focus and energy to the
external arena. The evolving active and revisionist foreign
policy soon became a corollary of the domestic reform
program, and the former's "radical" style was designed
primarily to mobilize the support of change-oriented elements
behind a president contending with conservative and status
quo interests at home.

Once the "philosophical" underpinnings of Echeverría's
foreign policy were for the most part coherently developed,
the emphasis switched to a conscious pursuit of objectives
which—to adapt Michael O'Leary's (1969: 325) generaliza-
tions concerning developing states to the Mexican case—
could not be obtained by changes effected at the margin of the

established international order. Hence, Echeverría's dissent against the prevailing international system was not merely a tactic to take the minds of his constituency off problems at home, nor was it simply an excuse for unfulfilled promises. He perceived a radical transformation of fundamental aspects of the international system as necessary for furnishing solutions to domestic problems and the national malaise.

Consequently, Echeverría used membership in the organizations of an unintegrated international system to promote that system's reconstruction into an integrated and just one. Like other weaker members of the international system, Mexico under Echeverría chose to present issues and initiatives in the widest possible forums, where prospects for mobilizing support against the stronger members held more promise.[1]

By focusing on the domestic sources and uses of Echeverría's foreign policy, a fuller understanding of its overall context, evolution, and dynamics can be gained. The body of literature, both Mexican and foreign, on the subject is still modest, although steadily growing.[2] Some studies purporting to deal with contemporary Mexican foreign policy fall short of expectations because they address themselves essentially to the pre-Echeverría epoch (e.g., Astiz, 1974), while most analyses lean heavily toward economic explanations in searching for motivations and foreign policy objectives (e.g., Poitras, 1974). This outlook is undoubtedly plausible, given the emphasis for several decades by Mexican administrations on economic issues in their international relations. Furthermore, agencies dealing with economic matters have joined the president and Ministry for Foreign Relations in dominating the institutional structure for formulating foreign policy. A dramatic testimony of this state of affairs was given by Echeverría himself in his fifth annual address to Congress and the nation (1975a): "The international policy — today more than ever — is part of the internal economic policy."

An attempt to trace the origins of Echeverría's new foreign policy to preceding administrations (Kaye, 1975), particularly to that of President Adolfo López Mateos (1958–1964), has been refuted (Hamilton, 1975). Instead, several analysts (e.g., Poitras, 1974: 65) acknowledge that Echeverría's own perceptions and personal style have largely shaped the course of events. That admission, however, is not followed up by an attempt to identify specific factors that may account for Echeverría's perceptions and performance, thus leaving many questions unanswered. The fact that Mexico is a developing nation internally and a dependent nation externally does not in itself explain Echeverría's foreign policy initiatives. One can legitimately argue that these basic "actor characteristics" typified Mexico long before Echeverría became president. It is true that internal economic developments—such as the country's growing external debt—gave increasing urgency to economic issues, and that developments in the global system and the regional (Latin American) subsystem made it possible to design new tactics to achieve traditional objectives. Yet, while Mexico's developmental impasse and external dependence are undoubtedly crucial in explaining the choice of foreign policy goals, they do not satisfactorily account for the innovations and "radical" style introduced by the Echeverría administration.

What is needed is a complementary examination of Echeverría's political experience and evolution, at least from the time of the Díaz Ordaz administration (1964–1970), when Echeverría held the key post of minister of the interior (*gobernación*), to the first and crucial years of his own *sexenio* (the six-year presidential term), when the course of his policies was being shaped. Role and situational factors, i.e., the impact of organizational and role experience, as well as a highly self-conscious perception of his public image, played an important part in influencing Echeverría's responses and decisions as president.

Hence, this study does not take issue with the economic interpretations, but rather offers a complementary angle that has tended to be overlooked by available analyses. After discussing the events that stimulated the linkage between internal political developments and the reformulation of Mexican foreign policy, and their impact on domestic and foreign affairs, this study will analyze the novel aspects of Echeverría's foreign policy and show how they departed from the established principles of Mexico's relations with the international community.

II. THE CATALYST FOR CHANGE: THE UNIVERSITY COMMUNITY'S PROTEST OF 1968

The 1968 events that rocked Mexico's society and polity were as traumatic for Mexican elites and citizens as they were surprising to those outside observers versed in Mexican politics. These generalized feelings largely surfaced because the severe disturbances happened — in the words of James N. Goodsell (1969: 31) of the *Christian Science Monitor* — "to a nation long considered Latin America's most stable and, in many ways, most progressive." The element of surprise was heightened by the fact that there had been sustained economic growth and a marked decline in university activism until 1966. The crisis that erupted in 1966 at the dominant National Autonomous University of Mexico (UNAM) was an intra-university one that only in retrospect appears to have contained some forewarning of later developments.

The growing realization that preceding events should be viewed as linked or contributing to the protests of 1968 is an outgrowth of the self-criticism and soul searching of post-1968 Mexican literature. Thus, several writers (Castillo, 1973; Moreno Sánchez, 1971; López Cámara, 1971) mark 1958 as the point of entry into a decade when domestic socioeconomic problems were intensified. Several long-range processes and developments exacerbated economic tensions and caused political frustrations, particularly among progressive and leftist circles. For example, a government document citing quantitative data openly admits to a significant increase in the inequality of national income distribution between 1950 and 1963. It also shows (Secretaría de Recursos Hidráulicos, 1973: 8–9) that with a GINI coefficient (an index measuring inequality of income distribution) of 0.55 in 1963, Mexico was trailing many Latin American countries, such as Argentina, Colombia, Panama, Costa Rica, Brazil, El Salvador, and Venezuela (with 0.46, 0.47, 0.48, 0.50, 0.52, 0.53, and 0.53, respectively).

Another development that had repercussions in 1968 is the short-lived experience of the National Liberation Movement (MLN). The merger of fragmented Communist, Marxist, and leftist elements into a unified front in 1961 was an attempt to create an independent electoral force of a nationalist-leftist orientation that would offer a viable alternative and genuine opposition to the ruling *Partido Revolucionario Institucional* (PRI). Although it enjoyed the support of ex-President Lázaro Cárdenas, the MLN failed to gain the recognition as a legal party that would have allowed it to participate in the 1964 presidential elections. This failure and the eventual demise of the MLN accentuated the difficulties of using this political option to effect changes at the national level or to challenge the PRI's power monopoly. At the personal level, the linkage to 1968 is even more visible, as some of the MLN veterans resurfaced that year. One of them was Heberto Castillo, a teacher at the National Polytechnic Institute and an important militant in 1968.[3]

Another factor that helped alienate progressive circles was the inflexible and conservative administration of President Gustavo Díaz Ordaz (1964–1970), who succeeded the more liberal and, on the whole, popular Adolfo López Mateos (1958–1964).

While all these causes contributed to the latent discontent that became manifest in the 1968 protest, the reactions of the Echeverría administration to that protest in the period after 1970 cannot be fully understood without an appreciation of the role played by the university community.[4]

In general terms, the activist university community of 1968 assumed the role of interest aggregation, or a transient political party, thereby competing with and partly substituting for the established national political parties. Such a process is facilitated when those structures that are expected to perform essential political functions fail to carry them out effectively because they are controlled by the elite. Consequently, pressure may mount for the creation of an alternate structure to replace those vacated roles, as indeed such pressure was building up in Mexico in the decade prior to 1968. Prompted by suitable environmental stimuli, that is, the advent of a "trigger"—an abrupt unifying issue in the form of a severe threat posed from outside—alliances formed, ranks closed, and the university community surged forth as the noncaptive structure that could "usurp" these functions, at least temporarily.

The dissident university community of 1968, both in the systemic function it fulfilled and in the responses it triggered from the regime, represents a sui generis phenomenon that is clearly distinct from other manifestations of protest that troubled Mexican politics in the decade preceding 1968 (e.g., the railroad workers' strike of 1958–1959, and the doctors' strike of 1964–1965). The students and their university-based allies rapidly developed a sense of community. In the absence of common professional-economic interests that motivated more homogeneous groups, however, the 1968 protest came to embrace a much wider range of political, social, and economic issues.

It can be argued that while the striking workers and doctors precipitated confrontations that were crises of control (in that they developed noncaptive interest group activity), the 1968 movement created a crisis of legitimacy. Hence, a substantial part of the elite's immediate response to the 1968 challenge took the shape of an antistudent, de-legitimation campaign that was not undertaken against the dissident "nonuniversity" groups.

The severe student disturbances that shook Mexico's capital in 1966 differed from those of 1968 in scope, style, and substance. The 1966 student strike ("Chávez Affair") is still the subject of varying interpretations. The most widely held view is that the students were manipulated by the Díaz Ordaz government in order to get rid of a political foe, Dr. Ignacio Chávez, the prestigious rector of the UNAM (Fagen and Cornelius, Jr., 1970: 297–336). Still, the grievances of 1966 essentially constituted a "reform movement" with an intra-university focus; the national significance was minimal and the challenge to the authorities negligible, in contrast to the alarming proportions of the 1968 movement. Yet, the 1966 conflict might be viewed as the formative mobilization experience for student activists and groups. Luis González de

14

Alba (1971: 22), a pivotal member of the top student coordinating organ during 1968, the National Strike Committee (*Consejo Nacional de Huelga* or CNH), considered the 1966 UNAM strike a landmark, heralding an era in which the "Left" within the National University gathered force and strove for greater politicization of the student body. In other words, 1966 demonstrated that a university crisis, manipulated by outside forces for political purposes, could backfire by triggering an intensive process of student politicization. This process gained momentum from environmental stimuli and eventually erupted as an autonomous, generalized protest. The student protest of 1968 was not a university reform movement and university problems as such (except for the issue of university autonomy) did not rank high on its agenda. It was unprecedented in modern Mexican history because it evolved into a general social protest which challenged — in a manner and intensity previously unknown — the very legitimacy of the country's power elite and the political, economic, and social structures controlled by that elite.

The 1968 student protest found expression in two separate and fundamentally different sets of demands. The first comprised the "facade," or the formal list of student grievances, while the other contained the more substantive issues. The official "six-points" manifesto was drafted in early August 1968, amid escalating student disturbances and heavy-handed police and army countermeasures. Although formulated well before the bloody climax of the student-government confrontation on October 2 at the Plaza de Tres Culturas in the Tlatelolco section of Mexico City, the central theme of the "six-points" list was an attack against the personal, legal, and institutional symbols of government repression. It included the following demands: freedom for political prisoners; dismissal of Mexico City's top police and *granaderos* (riot police) officers, Generals Luis Cueto and Raúl Mendiolea, and Lieutenant Colonel Armando Frías; elimination of the *granaderos* unit, "the direct instrument of repression"; annulment of Article 145 of the Penal Code (*delito de disolución social*), "the juridical instrument of aggression"; indemnification for the families of victims of the "aggression of July

26 and on"; and the determination of responsibility for the "acts of repression and vandalism of the authorities committed by the police, *granaderos,* and the army."[5]

Although unusually daring within the context of Mexican politics, the "six points" reflected a basically defensive and short-range position. A possible explanation for this relative moderation is that the list was adopted by the students' National Strike Committee, and thus represented the minimal consensus arrived at by the diverse activist groups at the time. Furthermore, the phrasing of the "official" demands allowed a number of university professors and intellectuals who had ties with the "establishment" to endorse them publicly. The movement's more aggressive, critical, and long-range aspect as a catalyst for sociopolitical protest was communicated via diverse media, often in an uncoordinated manner. The ample documentary evidence gathered by sympathetic "chroniclers" and interpreters, such as Ramón Ramírez (1969) and Elena Poniatowska (1971), unequivocally reveals the real targets of the student attacks (see also Carrión et al., 1969; Lenkersdorf, 1969; Goodsell, 1969; U.S. Committee for Justice, no date; and Liebman, 1971).

Many of the grievances contained demands for democratizing Mexican politics and making the political system more responsive and participatory. The students also called for the correction of social and economic injustices through a more equitable distribution of opportunities and national income. Specifically, they charged that:

● The lower social strata were alienated by a bourgeois elite that used "revolutionary" rhetoric to manipulate public opinion.

● Government control was exercised through a system of nonautonomous interest groups, and was strengthened by a loyal press and the lack of real interparty rivalry.

● There was a lack of syndicalist autonomy among the urban workers, as well as among the rural *campesinos,* both of whom were manipulated and controlled by PRI-affiliated unions.

● Though the government claimed to represent the working masses, its development policies and tax structure benefited "big business" and discriminated against wage earners.

● Political power was concentrated in the hands of a small group that obstructed attempts to weaken its monopoly.

● Unbiased information was unavailable, and the systematic frustration of efforts to organize independent political organizations—accompanied by occasional electoral frauds—fomented apathy and "marginalism" (Ramírez, 1969: 503-507).

From these charges, it is evident that the student protest attacked the inadequacies of all of Mexico's major political institutions. The nature of the charges also helps to explain why the student body emerged as a self-appointed interest aggregator for the socially, economically, and politically alienated of the country.

Since 1929, Mexico has been ruled by an authoritarian, monopolistic governing party, the PRI (and its earlier versions, the PNR and PRM). Three other officially sanctioned "opposition" parties, the PAN (*Partido de Acción Nacional*), PPS (*Partido Popular Socialista*), and PARM (*Partido Auténtico de la Revolución Mexicana*), give the regime the aura of a legitimate democracy by creating what critical Mexicans term a "simulated plurality" (Martínez de la Vega, 1971: 26–27). But a viable, free, and competitive multi-party system is still lacking. None of the official opposition parties takes a stance significantly more radical than does the PRI in its periodic vacillations between right and center, nor do they constitute a challenge of any consequence to the ruling party.

Reflecting on this state of affairs, one observer (Jacobson, 1975: 22) astutely describes the role played by the PRI in national politics: "The most important consideration is that the PRI is not really a political party in the traditional sense of a contender for power which may be in or out of office. Rather, the PRI was organized by the victors of an armed struggle as a bureaucratic device to preserve the peace and hold the power of the state in the hands of a self-perpetuating elite."

The major interest groups, particularly those representing the lower classes—for example, the Confederation of Mexican Workers (CTM) and the National Peasants' Confederation (CNC)—are integral parts of the government party and this status has placed them in a captive position. Many of the CTM's affiliated workers' syndicates are *sindicatos charros,* the Mexican term for unions run by a "sold-out" leadership. The ruthless treatment of union leader Demetrio Vallejo from 1958 to 1970 because of his nonconformist attitudes is an excellent example of how little syndicalist autonomy the regime has tolerated. The subservient Congress and the largely mercenary press complete the authoritarian picture.[6]

In this situation, the function of interest aggregation had to be assumed by a noncaptive, sociopolitical group. In Mexico during the second half of the 1960s, the only significant group that could serve, even temporarily, as an alternate structure was the university community.[7]

Among those Mexican writers and analysts commenting on the 1968 events, there is considerable agreement as to the general character of the movement and its principal aims. Octavio Paz (1970: 28–31) presents an interesting cross-national comparison, suggesting an analogy between the Mexican and Eastern European student protests of 1968. Both, he believes, were directed toward similar objectives, namely, the rejection of foreign domination and the aspiration for democratic reform.

It should be noted that there is no factual evidence supporting Paz's "anti-imperialist" thesis. A review of all "official" CNH declarations compiled by Ramón Ramírez reveals no serious anti-United States concerns on the part of the movement's directorate. Student criticism was predominantly directed toward internal matters and no attention was given to foreign policy orientation or the issue of dependence.

On the other hand, there is widespread agreement about the democratic nature of the movement. Victor Flores Olea, for instance, argues that by raising the banners of true representative democracy, the Mexican protesters differed profoundly from their non-Mexican counterparts of the late 1960s, such as the French students who agitated against all types of representation. He explains the 1968 movement's democratizing thrust by the fact that Mexico had never experienced a functioning democracy, while some veteran democracies were entering an advanced stage of crisis in their representative political institutions. Carlos Monsiváis (1971: 271, 273), Ramón Ramírez (1969: Vol. I, 23–28), and Elena

Poniatowska (1971: 20) also stress the democratic and constitutionalist spirit of the movement.

Francisco López Cámara (1971) and Manuel Moreno Sánchez (1971) differ on the nature of the class background to the student protest. While the former sees the students as spearheading middle-class discontent, the latter gives more weight to lower-class alienation as the prelude to 1968. Nevertheless, both tend to agree on the movement's ultimate goals, either as reformist, democratizing, and constitutionalist (Moreno Sánchez), or as directed at revamping the system to accommodate middle-class aspirations (López Cámara). Similar views have been advanced by Jorge Carrión and Fernando Carmona (1969), Javier Barros Sierra (1972: 123–134), the UNAM's rector during 1968, and movement activists Luis González de Alba (1971) and Heberto Castillo (1973).

To carry on an effective protest, the students attempted to organize, mobilize support, and communicate their demands with maximum impact. The ultimate test was their ability to break through the communications barrier and enlist popular support outside the university community. For its part, the government acted harshly to frustrate these moves and in the process firmly demonstrated its control over most of the country's mass organizations and interest structures, as well as the Congress and the bulk of the national press.

The university community, under the direction of the National Strike Committee, employed diverse tactics to relay its message to the public. The most spectacular were the mass protest marches, such as those held in Mexico City in August 1968. While the students did not shy away from acting openly and in large numbers, they also operated in small groups to enlist the support of, politicize, and build sympathy with the lower classes. This semiclandestine task was carried out by "political brigades" working in lower-class neighborhoods, who at times even utilized rides on popular bus lines and convened "lightning meetings" for "blitz" propaganda operations. Attempts to mobilize support from laborers at work sites were frustrated by swift government action, and many arrests were made. Compared to their work among industrial laborers and urban dwellers, the students' activism among *campesinos* was slight (Poniatowska, 1971: 44–46).

Because they sought any possible public forum to express their views, the students tried unsuccessfully to force the government into an open, preferably televised, dialogue. Their failure to mobilize significant support among the lower class was reflected in the progovernment declarations issued by the country's major worker and peasant organizations (the CTM and CNC). Even the central figure of the Mexican Left, ex-President Lázaro Cárdenas, maintained a proestablishment stance by condemning manifestations of student violence (El Día, October 6, 1968). The co-opted "opposition" party of Vicente Lombardo Toledano, the PPS, demonstrated its loyalty more diligently by issuing a passionate statement against the "antinational provocation." The few statements released by the PAN mildly criticized the government, expressed a half-hearted and qualified understanding of the students, and sidestepped the real issues. This lack of clear-cut commitment, if not timidity, was reflected in vague wording and the censuring of both government repression and the abuses of power by corrupt student leaders and organizations (Ramírez, 1969: Vol. I, 116–117; Vol. II, 100–101, 178–181).

Criticism of the government was rarely heard from major political figures; the prominent *Priistas* Carlos Madrazo, ex-governor of Tabasco and former president of the PRI, and Manuel Moreno Sánchez, a liberal former Senate leader, were exceptions. It would be erroneous to conclude, however, that the students did not enjoy widespread sympathy among the general public, but simply that open expressions of support, on the whole, were spontaneous or represented marginal groups and organizations.

The noncompromising and repressive measures adopted by the government in response to the university community's challenge were accompanied by an intensive media campaign aimed at discrediting the movement in the eyes of the public. Hostile public opinion would help support the security forces' intimidation and punitive actions. Thus, by using mass media and loyal mass organizations, the goverment skillfully manipulated popular opinion and sentiments to deflate and illegitimize the student protests. In his address of September 1, 1968, President Díaz Ordaz appealed for "law and order." A speech delivered by General Alfonso Corona del Rosal, regent of the Federal District, to transport and cleaning workers also invoked the appeal to "law and order" and is an instructive example of mass psychology:

> I had true satisfaction in accepting your kind invitation to accompany you on this occasion, because I have known for many years the spirit of struggle, self-denial, and sacrifice of you all . . . you have always been ready to defend the unity of the Mexican people . . . you are the poor sector of the capital, but as has always been done by the poor sector of our fatherland, you are the first ones who want to cooperate for the aggrandizement of Mexico. . . . We need tranquility, we need peace . . . peace in which economic improvement is being sought, above all for the most humble. . . . Who is favored by the disorder in our fatherland? . . . nobody is favored by the disorder in our fatherland, and those who are hurt most by it are the poor (El Día, August 9, 1968).

In other instances, "anti-intellectual" tones underlay attacks against the students. They were accused of striving for undeserved prerogatives reminiscent of the colonial *"fueros,"* and of placing themselves above the law and the common citizen in their demands for university autonomy. Accusations of immorality also figured in the antistudent campaign. The most powerful tactic, however, was the appeal to deeply rooted nationalistic and xenophobic sentiments, which depicted the students as unpatriotic and even dangerous to "national security."[8] A conspicuous instance of the manipulation of patriotic feelings is the celebrated "flag incident" (*acto de desagravio*) of August 28. In a mass loyalty ceremony organized by the government, the national flag was reinstated at the Zócalo, where the day before students had replaced it with their red and black strike banner.[9]

A variety of "conspiracy theories," placing the blame upon various "subversive" elements, either foreign or local or both, flourished that year. A case in point is an elaborate "explanation" of the crisis by Raul Prieto (El Día, August 7, 1968), which alleged that the FBI and the CIA had collaborated with

Mexican reactionaries in an attempt to "expose" the role of Cuban "agents" in the student movement and thereby bring about a break in diplomatic relations between Mexico and Cuba. Needless to say, this alleged "rightist conspiracy" had its counterpart in the form of an alleged "leftist plot" (López Portillo, 1968). The government tried to give credence to such rumors by detaining five "prominent members" of the Mexican Communist party (PCM) for investigation into their roles in the student disturbances. The authorities also claimed to have proof that the PCM and its student front organization, the CNED, had organized "shock units" to provoke disorder and to aggravate student-police clashes (Revista de la Universidad de México, July 20, 1968: 5).

III. THE ECHEVERRIA RESPONSE: DOMESTIC POLITICS

The question of the regime's ability effectively to accommodate new demands has been a major test for the Mexican political system. Two stages may be discerned in the government's response to the students' challenge. The first, characterized by repression, extended from the crisis in 1968 to the close of the Díaz Ordaz administration in 1970. Several underlying factors determined the government's response during this period. The novel demands contained in the university community's protest were too extensive and far-reaching to permit short-range accommodation. At the same time, student dissent was seen as a major threat to the elite's legitimacy. The president of the republic, a traditionally revered figure and arch-pillar of political authority, had become a target for ruthless and offensive student attacks. The "revolutionary" character of the regime, its principal legitimizing "ideology," had been mocked.

Even worse, the possibility that the university community's protest might affect other segments of Mexican society harbored grave dangers to those in power. By inculcating a sense of the elite's illegitimacy and by attempting to politicize Mexico City's lower strata, the students threatened the stability of the regime. They fostered mobilization of that segment of the populace characterized by attributes of a "subject" political culture — political passivity, if not docility. Since its examination in studies of Mexican political culture (Almond and Verba, 1963; Scott, 1965; Kahl, 1968), this segment has been considered an important factor in accounting for the country's relative political tranquility. Had significant numbers of the "subject" sector, regularly providing "diffuse support for the system through their attachment to its revolutionary symbolism and manifest goals" (Hansen, 1971: 187), been dissuaded from their customary allegiances to join the students, the protest movement would have assumed an ominous, new dimension.

Further aggravating the confrontation were the preparations then under way for the 1968 Olympic Games to be held late that year. The government's credibility and Mexico's national prestige were therefore at stake. These perceived dangers provoked the harsh government reaction—physical repression, the de-legitimizing campaign, and efforts to isolate the students from the public at large.

The second stage originated with the administration of President Luis Echeverría. In this phase there were clear indications of new policy trends, namely, attempts to lower the repressive profile of the regime and to improve its adaptiveness. These changes were motivated by personal considerations, as well as by the survival instincts of the governing elite. The PRI's showing in the 1970 presidential elections was alarming indeed: 34 percent of the eligible voters abstained, 25 percent of the ballots cast were annulled, and another 20 percent favored other parties (Pereyra, 1974: 59). A reevaluation of government policies was imperative.

In effect, Echeverría's new style and political orientation had already begun to surface during his hectic electoral campaign. Throughout the eight months following his selection as the PRI's candidate in 1969, he criss-crossed the country in a vigorous and untiring series of preelection speeches and meetings, expounding his intentions and ideas. He thus broke a PRI convention: traditionally, a candidate does not demonstrate an independent course until sworn in as president (Cosío Villegas, 1974: 16). In so doing, Echeverría not only undermined the power and authority of the incumbent president during the last year of Díaz Ordaz's term, but at the same time tried to dissociate himself from the cumbersome political legacy of the 1968 crisis. There is little doubt that as president, Echeverría wished to rid himself of the "stigma of Tlatelolco," which had haunted him since his days as secretary of the interior in 1968, and that he desired to create a progressive-liberal image for himself. Therefore, his administration generally tried to accommodate the widespread discontent which had intensified since 1968.

The most obvious manifestation of dissatisfaction was the rise of the urban guerrillas in Mexico, who were joined in some cases by student extremists and even young university lecturers.[10] This new challenge culminated in the kidnapping of the president's father-in-law, José Guadalupe Zuno, who was held as a hostage from August 20 to September 8, 1974. The FRAP, the guerrilla group that claimed responsibility for the action, called it *Operación Tlatelolco, 2 de octubre de 1968*, an unsubtle reminder. The upsurge of guerrilla activism was usually met by a strong government response, from the arresting of militants to the ousting of five Soviet diplomats after it was discovered that a group of Mexican students had used the Soviet Union as a transfer station on their way to North Korea for guerrilla training. To these measures one might add the still obscure automobile accident that caused the death of Genaro Vázquez Rojas, head of the MAR, seemingly the most important of the proliferating guerrilla organizations (MAR, FAR, FUZ, CAP, etc.). In late 1974, the Defense Ministry confirmed the death of the other *guerrillero* of national renown, Lucio Cabañas, who—according to an official version— was shot during a skirmish with the army in the troublesome state of Guerrero, where he had been operating since 1967.

Of greater significance is a wide range of policy measures the government undertook to distribute national income more equitably, provide social benefits to the poor, and liberalize the political process, as well as overtures made by the regime to the university and intellectual communities. Many of these policies clearly responded to the university community's sociopolitical critique of 1968 and to its role in the national political process.

A multifaceted strategy was developed to deal with the phenomenon of an increasingly politicized and dissent-prone university community, focusing primarily on the UNAM as the backbone and catalyst of any nationally significant and politically threatening student movement. Conciliatory moves—highlighted by Echeverría's daring visit to the UNAM campus in March 1975 for the first time since 1968— were coupled with structural and personnel changes, including replacing rectors at the UNAM and inaugurating a vigorous reform and development scheme for higher education. The main purpose of this scheme was to reduce the UNAM's weight in the national educational system.

The first signal to usher in the new liberalized political era was the general amnesty of imprisoned leaders of the 1968 movement, ordered by Echeverría early in 1971. Furthermore, the president issued a declaration of intent to open a dialogue with the Left, and coined the slogan *Apertura democrática* ("Democratic Opening"). In other words, the government became more permissive and open to criticism. In this atmosphere the press grew more daring and critical after 1971. Still, freedom of the press was only partial and selective, as is demonstrated by the closing of the proguerrilla weekly *Por Qué?* (September 1974) and the firing of *Excelsior's* editor and senior staff members (July 1976). Considerably greater leeway was granted to the nonviolent, nonestablishment Left, and major figures among critical non-*Priista* leftists have been permitted public expression.

Although some prominent activists of the 1968 movement were eventually co-opted by the government,[11] others took advantage of the relaxation of political controls to organize new leftist parties and campaigned successfully for support among workers and peasants. The first such grouping made its debut as early as November 1971, under the leadership of Heberto Castillo and Demetrio Vallejo. Its first national convention in August 1974 founded the Mexican Workers' party (PMT). The president's son Pablo attended the PMT convention, which was widely publicized. In 1973, a splinter group broke away from the Castillo-Vallejo camp to form the Socialist Workers' party (PST). Both groups tried unsuccessfully to obtain the legal registration that would have qualified them for the 1976 presidential elections.

Important personnel changes of political significance have taken place. Prominent among these were the oustings of Federal District Regent Alfonso Martínez Domínguez and Attorney General Julio Sánchez Vargas, following the scandalous *Halcones* incident of June 10, 1971, which will be discussed later in this chapter. On this occasion, Echeverría's image-building drive and prostudent public opinion combined to produce a decision that would have been unthinkable in

1968. In February 1972, Jesús Reyes Haroles, a publicist and former teacher at the UNAM, and Enrique González Pedrero, ex-director of the Faculty of Political and Social Sciences of the UNAM, were chosen as president and secretary general, respectively, of the PRI's National Executive Committee. This move infused new blood into the party's leadership, and further signaled the government's desire to improve communication with intellectuals and confer greater credibility and respectability on the PRI.

The administration introduced several institutional and procedural reforms into the basic "mechanics" of Mexican democracy. These meaures were primarily aimed at effecting changes in three interrelated spheres: on the intraparty level, or within the PRI; on the interparty level, by regulating and strengthening the role of the official opposition parties; and on the level of the electoral process as a whole, by updating and liberalizing some of its other aspects.

The PRI national caucus convened twice (March 1971 and 1972) to approve a new Declaration of Principles and Action Program, as well as to modify party statutes. Although these changes were officially heralded as a "reorganization of the ruling party" (Office of the President, 1972: 7), such an appraisal has not been universally accepted. In his first treatise on the Echeverría administration, historian D. Cosío Villegas (1973: 90–92) attributed these changes to the president's thinking rather than to intraparty deliberations. He maintained that their spirit was essentially conservative and that the measure introducing the secret ballot for representatives on local party committees was accompanied by few other innovations, thus falling far short of expectations. Some foreign "Mexico watchers" put it even more bluntly, arguing that the party remained "as unrepresentative as ever" and that the practice of "finger appointments" (*dedazo*) was still very much in evidence (Riding, 1973a).

The reforms concerning the opposition parties should not be understood as a fundamental restructuring of the system. As pointed out by political analyst Rafael Segovia, the promoters intended to achieve only limited legal reform, well within the boundaries of the existent framework, and to revitalize some of the system's saliently dysfunctional elements (Segovia, 1974: 52). While the continued operation of a parliamentary opposition was indispensable for providing the system with democratic legitimation, expanding interparty competition beyond the established quadruple "arrangement" was not contemplated. For the first time, however, according to Segovia, there was an effort to move from a regime dominated by one party with no effective parliamentary opposition to one in which such opposition could play some role in the lower house (*Cámara de Diputados*), be organized freely under the Constitution, and be firmly anchored in the electoral laws.

Segovia also observed that the reformers hoped to confine interparty conflicts within ideological terms and channel oppositional activity into the officially sanctioned parties. Underlying the electoral reforms was the fear that the PRI might be left without its weak and convenient "opponents." In this respect, a functioning opposition—ineffective as it might be—would serve as an essential support for the system. Accordingly, various legal measures made it easier for the opposition parties to campaign, inspect the electoral process, and gain a foothold in the federal legislature.

The electoral law of 1973 provided that the national opposition parties be represented on committees and boards of those elections in which they participated, and thus introduced at least a partial check against electoral frauds. The law granted the official opposition parties access to the mass media for the first time. The use of radio and television for campaigning greatly facilitated the exposure of voters to non-PRI propaganda, including those in vast rural areas who had never heard anything but the official line.

A major amendment lowered the minimum of the total vote required of an opposition party for entry into the Chamber of Deputies from the previous 2.5 to a mere 1.5 percent. The number of deputies allowed to represent an opposition party in the chamber was increased to a maximum of twenty-five. Lowering the entry requirement confirmed the weakness of the legal opposition, particularly the PARM and the PPS.

The deliberate strengthening of the small minority parties revealed the elite's preference for continuing the apparently pluralistic structure of the political party system, rather than making a transition to a bipartisan system that would leave the *Acción Nacional* as the only contender facing the PRI. Such a transition would polarize national politics and limit the electoral options, consequently improving the PAN's capability to garner the protest vote. A principal aim of the reform was therefore to solidify the parliamentary Left, which was electorally ineffectual but ideologically and symbolically useful (Segovia, 1974: 54).

Indeed, the results of the congressional elections of July 1973 primarily favored the two minor opposition parties, the PPS and PARM, and thus achieved in the short run the limited objectives embodied in the reform. As Segovia sees it, however, the drawback to the kind of systemic support provided by the official opposition parties is that the largest of the three, the PAN, has often threatened to withdraw from the race, while the smaller two have yet to offer a genuine opposition—over the years, they have almost always supported the PRI's presidential candidate.

Another amendment introduced by Echeverría prior to the 1973 congressional elections was the lowering of the age requirement for deputies from twenty-five to twenty-one years and for senators from thirty-five to thirty years, a move considered a special gesture to the younger generation to facilitate its absorption into the system.

A major target of the democratization efforts of the Echeverría administration was the entrenched leadership of Mexico's captive unions, or the *liderazgo charro*. The confrontation that ensued produced one of the most noteworthy political phenomena of the Echeverría *sexenio*—the rise to political power of the workers' syndicates organized through the CTM. This unintentional outcome demonstrated not only the tenuousness of Echeverría's power base, but also that some widely held postulates concerning the power and omnipotence of a Mexican president could be seriously challenged. The president was unable to override the resistance of major interest groups, which forced him to reconsider tactics and modify policies.

From the beginning of the *sexenio,* there was a noticeable intensification of press attacks against the *sindicatos charros* affiliated with the CTM. These attacks, directed mainly at the principal *charro* leader, CTM Secretary General Fidel Velázquez, were given official encouragement.[12] Velázquez had served uninterruptedly as secretary general of the CTM since 1941. Under his control, the Workers' Confederation became a docile organization that helped maintain and legitimize the system, functions that were extremely valuable to the elite. The "cleanup" and renovation of the unions, which the government envisaged as important manifestations of the *Apertura* policy, encountered stiff and militant opposition from the veteran *cetemista* cadres. Thus, the years from 1972 through early 1974 witnessed strained relations between the government and this group, except for occasional tactical lulls.

The government policy of encouraging independent unions in order to undermine the Velázquez group (through dissident syndicalist leaders like Rafael Galván, Valentín Campa, and others) never gained sufficient momentum to topple the durable Fidel. In this power struggle, Velázquez used popular demands (including a forty-hour work week, significant salary hikes, and national unemployment insurance), as well as pressure tactics (threatening a general strike on four occasions and mass solidarity demonstrations like the one held in Cuernavaca on October 8, 1972), to rally worker support and convert the CTM into an effective pressure group. He not only asserted a new degree of CTM autonomy and power and rebuilt his own image as the workingman's champion, but he also outmaneuvered his opponents in the syndicates and the government. That he had gained the upper hand became evident in April 1974, when the CTM's National Congress reelected him to his seventh consecutive term as secretary general.

At that stage, de-escalation of the conflict with President Echeverría was almost inevitable. Furthermore, early in 1975 the process of selecting the PRI candidate for the 1976 presidential elections was set in motion. Facing the prospect of intraparty struggle for the succession, the president could not write off the support of a political force such as the CTM. The very fate of his fledgling reform policies was at stake. At the same time, the CTM was interested in staving off any attempt by rightist forces to advance a conservative candidate who would reverse the course of the "revolution." These converging interests set the stage for reconciliation. The Echeverría administration initiated several fiscal and welfare measures to attenuate income inequality. Here, his co-optation of the university community's criticism in 1968 was most pronounced. In his sixth and last annual message to the nation, Echeverría (1976) presented his government's social policy record in language reminiscent of the National Strike Committee leaflets. A particularly striking section of his address was:

> It is in their social policy that the governments resulting from a revolution test their legitimacy and efficacy. . . . In 1970, the essential constitutional provisions on the egalitarian distribution of wealth and justice in collective relations had been seriously disregarded. With the abandonment of the principles and deviation from the objectives an extremely individualistic mentality was cultivated and we became the victims of ideological infiltration whose supreme sign of success is the enrichment of a minority at the expense of exploiting other men.

In this sphere of economic redistribution, the establishment of INFONAVIT (National Workers' Housing Fund Institute) figured prominently. Created by Article 136 of the New Reformed Federal Labor Law, INFONAVIT is financed by a special levy on all businesses — 5 percent of their workers' salaries. In its first year of operation (1973–1974), the program was designed to build 100,000 low-cost housing units, then 28.5 percent of the 350,000 units required annually (Journal of Commerce, June 7, 1973). Among other institutions established to channel resources to low-income families was the National Fund of Development and Guarantees for Working Consumers (FONACOT). In less than two years FONACOT distributed credits amounting to three billion pesos to 420,000 families of workers (Echeverría, 1976). In addition, social security payments by companies were increased significantly and the program's coverage was vastly expanded. According to Echeverría's sixth *Informe presidencial*, the number of people covered by social security increased during his administration from 11,119,000 to 25,020,000.

The government's experience with three experiments in fiscal reform in the period 1971–1975 demonstrated the political constraints binding an aggressive economic redistribution policy. The Fiscal Reform Bill of 1971 attempted to increase tax rates for the upper brackets (to a maximum of 42 percent versus the previous 32 percent), as well as to raise rates on fixed incomes from bonds and securities. Its formulation was altered, however, by pressure from the private industrial-commercial community, and thus the high-income groups were only marginally affected. In early 1973, further efforts by the government to expand its income base once more encountered resistance from the private sector, resulting in the modification of some important proposals (Análisis Político, September 30, 1973: 4).

Continuing inflation and an increasing external debt prompted the government to embark upon its third fiscal reform, which went into effect in 1975.[13] But once again opposition from the private sector succeeded in significantly reducing the redistributive character of the legislation. Unwilling or unable seriously to challenge the business community, the government chose its tactics accordingly. By increasing luxury taxes and further raising the income tax ceiling from 42 to 50 percent (Excelsior, September 20, 1974), the reform primarily affected the middle class, which was too weakly organized to muster the influence to block it.[14]

Despite the government's avoidance of direct taxation on the private business sector and criticism to the effect that the president's solution to the problem of just income distribution was merely to call for a rise in productivity (Cosío Villegas, 1973: 92), Echeverría's fiscal policy does represent a departure from previous patterns. During former administrations, tax policies affected mostly workers and wage earners who could not evade payment. Under Echeverría, the tax base was expanded to include higher levels of income. According to the president (1976), the national fiscal burden (taxes as a proportion of the total GNP) "increased from its former static level of 2.5 percent of the gross national product to over 16 percent in 1975." The new tax reforms, therefore, were welcomed by the worker and peasant sectors, as well as by the business community, while the middle class protested loudly but ineffectively (Análisis Político, November 4 and 11, 1974).

Various moves were made to placate the "intellectual community" and other critics. These comprised granting the *Premio Nacional* to Daniel Cosío Villegas, expanding the *Colegio Nacional* to include "younger" figures such as Carlos Fuentes, and inviting several intellectuals and "independent" press personalities to join the presidential entourage on official trips abroad.

Some of the diplomatic appointments made by the president went beyond the customary policy of appointing non-career diplomats to ambassadorial posts. In early 1975, Echeverría named Carlos Fuentes, one of the initial supporters of the dissident Castillo-Vallejo group in 1971, ambassador to Paris and the UNAM's Victor Flores Olea to represent Mexico in Moscow. Olea's critical analysis of the 1968 crisis had been circulated nationally after its publication in *Siempre* on March 15, 1972.

Echeverría devoted considerable time to cultivating intellectuals, students, and teachers through *audiencias* and receptions in his office or at the official residence, *Los Pinos*. Cosío Villegas (1974: 119–120) observed that the greatest number of visits (excluding diplomats and foreign personalities) was made by this group.

Education Minister Victor Bravo Ahuja trimmed the power of the UNAM by decentralizing its educational resources. The vastly expanded demand for higher education has been partially accommodated by the creation of new institutions, largely independent of the UNAM. Thus, in 1973 the Ministry of Education founded its own system of *Colegios de Bachilleres,* and in 1974 a rival major university, the *Universidad Autónoma Metropolitana* (UAM), was established in the capital. The UNAM itself created new interdisciplinary preparatory colleges, *Colegios de Ciencias y Humanidades,* dispersed among five campuses throughout the Federal District. Furthermore, existing private universities, such as the Catholic *Ibero-Americana,* have expanded significantly since 1968, offering additional options to circumvent the UNAM (Latin America, August 16, 1974: 250, 252).

Yet another facet of this overall strategy has been the great impetus given to CONACYT (National Council for Science and Technology) to expand the country's scientific-technological infrastructure in order to accommodate the increasing numbers of graduates pouring out of Mexico's academic institutions.

Echeverría's personal involvement with the student movement as secretary of the interior in 1968, and his confrontation with repercussions of the crisis as president of Mexico after December 1970, made him—even more than his predecessor—the "president of the student crisis." The university community, which in 1968 acted as a transient semipolitical party, had an undeniable impact on a wide range of policies promulgated by the Echeverría administration. That there has been such an impact—the full extent of which is still undetermined[15] — was due in no small measure to Echeverría himself.

Whether or not, as critics suggest, Echeverría's political initiatives constituted modest and essentially "stylish" changes rather than structural reforms, the president worked for the continuation of reform beyond the period of his own term in office by influencing the choice of a successor. Here the president masterminded a strategy that introduced a substantive change in the most crucial, and until recently most guarded, of Mexican political processes, the presidential succession. Echeverría charged his minister of water resources, L. Rovirosa Wade, with publicly announcing (on April 11, 1975) the names of all PRI presidential aspirants (*pre candidatos*). This early move was widely regarded as putting an end to the long-established tradition of *tapadismo,* that is, concealment by innermost party circles of the selection process (Madrazzo, 1975). Publicly naming the precandidates served two fundamental, though seemingly contradictory, purposes—control and democratization. Control

34

was furthered by limiting the competition to a small number of approved precandidates, increasing predictability, and preventing last-minute surprises. But the precandidates were also expected to make their political views known to the public (Madrazzo, 1975), an innovation that could legitimately be presented as an impressive accomplishment of the president's *Apertura* policy. Exposure of the process and the contenders to public scrutiny signified the partial democratization of a hitherto nondemocratic practice at the crux of the system.

Nevertheless, Echeverría's reform program encountered serious difficulties because, during much of his *sexenio,* he had few allies. He enjoyed the support of the controlled *campesino* sector (CNC), the anti-Velázquez segments of the trade unions, and the progressive "press cliques" such as *Siempre, El Día,* and, to a certain extent, *Excelsior.* This base was fortified by patronage appointments to ranking party, federal, and state government positions, as well as by the many new and younger personalities elected as PRI deputies to the national legislature in July 1973.

Relations with other important groups remained strained and even antagonistic. Echeverría clashed with private business over such issues as the deflationary policy and the cutbacks in public spending, which produced the economic slowdown of 1971; government support of trade union demands for large wage increases; the rising pace of inflation; the increasing terrorism and kidnappings of business magnates by urban guerrillas; and the pro-Allende foreign policy.

The private sector's opposition was occasionally spearheaded by the industrialists and business interests of Monterrey (for example, the one-day business strike of June 1974 organized by the Monterrey Chamber of Commerce). The hard core of the powerful "Monterrey group," which operates from the populous, highly industrialized capital of the northern state of Nuevo León, has been the Garza Sada family. The head of the family, Eugenio Garza Sada, was assassinated in September 1973 at the age of 82. The fact that the president found it politically expedient to travel to Monterrey to pay his last respects was a telling indication of the power wielded by this group. Echeverría's presence at the funeral did not deter the family representative from harshly attacking the federal government in his eulogy. His accusations were seconded by the presidents of the national confederations representing private industrial and commercial interests, the CONCAMIN and CONCANACO (García, 1973b; Garibay, 1973). Another group with whom relations remained belligerent until 1974 was the old guard syndicalist leadership. In addition, the middle sectors were irritated by the government's fiscal policies. As for the university community, the hostile reception it accorded Echeverría during his 1975 visit to the UNAM showed that the president was not fully "rehabilitated" at the most dominant and most politicized Mexican university.

The disagreements between Echeverría and the conservative wing of his own party erupted in a confrontation between the president and his arch-rival, Alfonso Martínez Domínguez. The clash was precipitated by the *Halcones* affair of 1971 and ended with the ousting of Martínez Domínguez from his government post. But it was only after an attempt to bring him back to power as governor of the state of Nuevo León had been successfully blocked (in December 1972) that the demise of Martínez Domínguez was complete.

The *Halcones* affair constituted a severe internal crisis and merits further elaboration at this point. It was destined to embarrass the president, as well as to weaken the democratizing political role of the UNAM and radical segments of the larger university community.

On Corpus Christi Day, June 10, 1971, student leaders and fellow travelers (e.g., PCM militant Marcue Pardiñas) called their first unauthorized large-scale antigovernment demonstration in the capital since the protests of 1968. It was initiated by the COCO (*Comité coordinador de los comités de lucha*), an interuniversity leftist action group and distant heir to the defunct CNH, partly to express solidarity with students at the University of Nuevo León who were then engaged in a conflict over the issue of university autonomy. As the eight to ten thousand students marched toward the center of Mexico City, they were attacked by a force of some five hundred young thugs armed with sticks and firearms. A savage clash resulted in which, by conservative estimates, eleven students died, twenty-two disappeared, and up to two hundred were injured (New York Times, June 20, 1971; for more, see Excelsior and El Heraldo de México, June 11, 1971). The attack unleashed a power struggle that presented the gravest challenge to Echeverría's reformist designs of his first six months in office.

The rampaging thugs, known as *los Halcones* ("the Hawks"), were clearly well organized and trained. Journalists who witnessed the incident produced evidence pointing to collusion between the police and the *Halcones*. Students exhibited recordings of radio messages exchanged between police officials and the attackers. Police and army units present at the scene maintained they had orders not to intervene; but as a result of this "neutrality," the *Halcones* were allowed to pass through a police cordon to carry out their attack. The police did not even intervene when some *Halcones* burst into a hospital (where injured students were being treated) to continue the brutal beatings.

Sources close to the president indicated to the media that there was evidence of collaboration between the Mexico City police and the *Halcones*. They implicated the regent of the Federal District and former president of the PRI, Alfonso Martínez Domínguez, who is said to have cooperated with conservative elements opposed to Echeverría's progressive policies (New York Times, June 14, 1971). Similarly, students and reporters insisted that the *Halcones* were trained and paid by the Federal District's police and municipal authorities, that they used regulation police weapons, and that they were transported in municipal vehicles on Corpus Christi Day (New York Times, June 17 and 20, 1971; Washington Post, July 16, 1971; El Universal, June 12 and July 13, 1971; Ultimas Noticias, June 12, 1971; Excelsior, June 13, 1971; El Heraldo de México, June 15, 1971).

The general interpretation of the June 10 events was that the *Halcones'* operation was sponsored by right-wing opponents of Echeverría in order to provoke student rioting and force him to repress the Left. In any event, the use of repressive measures against student demonstrators would discredit him in the progressive camp. The unleashing of the *Halcones* — an irregular force created during the presidency of Gustavo Díaz Ordaz (1964–1970) and under the "regency" of A. Corona del Rosal of the Federal District — was a shrewd maneuver to make it most difficult for the president to disclaim responsibility (New York Times, July 24, 1971; see also Latin America, June 18 and 25, 1971). It should be noted that a different interpretation suggested that the president had prior knowledge of the *Halcones'* operation, but took advantage of the ensuing public indignation to dispose of some political opponents (Washington Post, July 16, 1971). Still other critics (Oposición, June 15–30, 1973; Por Qué?, September 1971; Medina Valdés, 1972), from both the Left and Right, accused Echeverría of outright responsibility for the affair.

The forced resignations of Martínez Domínguez and Mexico City's Chief of Police Flores Curiel less than a week after the incident were a partial victory for Echeverría over his opponents in party, government, and business circles. The president promised a thorough investigation into the case; but, although Attorney General Sánchez Vargas, whom Echeverría had put in charge of the investigation, was forced out of office for failing to identify those responsible for the *Halcones* operation, the culprits were never officially unmasked. That the investigation was eventually suppressed testified not only to the power exercised by conservative anti-Echeverría elements, but also to the inability of any establishment faction to open such a Pandora's box without seriously endangering the position and prestige of the entire "revolutionary" family (Garibay, 1971). Publication of the results of the investigation would implicate high government and party officials and run counter to the established practice of thrashing out conflicts between elite factions behind closed doors.

In an editorial in *Excelsior,* Enrique Maza (1972) offered several explanations, none of them mutually exclusive, for the government's silence about the Corpus Christi affair. He proposed that the incident was the work of "powerful factions," strong enough to threaten the political stability and success of Echeverría's administration; thus, it became necessary to arrive at an accommodation with these elements, the price of which was the suppression of the investigation. Maza also suggested the possible complicity of a "prominent member" of the regime. Finally, in a variation on the first theme, he regarded the incident as an attempt by right-wing economic interests to intimidate the reform-bent president; the government's acquiescence in halting the investigation demonstrated its weakness vis-à-vis these interests.

Furthermore, the failure of the president to carry out the promised inquiry into the *Halcones* affair cast doubts on the sincerity of his liberal intentions and remained a challenge to his authority and credibility among radical critics (Por Qué?, June 21 and September 23, 1971; Punto Crítico, June 6, 1972, May 17, 1973).

Similar intraelite struggles arose over several gubernatorial nominations. In Sonora the president promoted Carlos Armando Biebrich, a trusted young university lecturer who had served as undersecretary of the interior, to block the candidacy of a PRI conservative (December 1972). In Veracruz in 1974 the president's forces were pitted against PRI right-wingers, while the same year in Michoacán the conflict involved leftist elements grouped around Lázaro Cárdenas's son, the dissident Cuauhtémoc Cárdenas. In both cases, the president's preference prevailed. Also in 1974, gubernatorial politicking in Hidalgo embroiled rival PRI groupings in an open struggle, and the party nominee (later replaced) was not the president's man (for more, see Latin America, November 29, 1974). Yet, in two other important states, governors who were identified with strong conservative interests were forced out of office after clashing with their local state universities (Eduardo Elizondo of Nuevo León in July 1971 and G. Bautista O'Farril of Puebla in May 1973).

The president's constant efforts to maneuver and readjust policies were reflected in unprecedented ministerial turnovers during his administration. In fact, all the secretaries heading the key economic ministries—including Finance, Industry and Commerce, Natural Resources, Labor, and Agriculture—were replaced.

These cumulative incidents appear to substantiate the proposition that the president's original base of support was narrow, a factor that limited the scope of his reformism. Precisely because of the dearth of public support, the confidence of the intellectual and university communities became all the more important to Echeverría. Within this sector, however, the UNAM remained a problematic "island"; it required special treatment and a policy designed to neutralize its political influence. The UNAM continued to serve as a stage for political conflicts, primarily during 1972 and 1973, when the paralyzing strikes of the *Normalistas* and the UNAM's employee syndicates resulted in a change of rectors.

IV. THE COMPENSATION: AN ACTIVIST-"RADICAL" FOREIGN POLICY

Objective Factors Behind Foreign Policy Reevaluation

As was briefly mentioned in the introductory chapter, several fundamental changes affecting Mexico's economic position, as well as developments at the regional level and within the international system at large, broke the ground for possible changes in its foreign policy. By chance, these processes converged with Luis Echeverría's assumption of the presidency. In this respect, some of the basic trends that led toward a reevaluation of foreign policy would probably have had a similar impact on any Mexican administration, regardless of the identity of the chief executive.

It was not until the late 1960s that the economic problems pertinent to Mexico's interaction with other nations became critical. The inadequacy of a strategy for industrial development based on import substitution and the ever-growing need for imported capital goods and foreign technology — which left their mark on a deteriorating balance of payments— demanded vigorous promotion of Mexican exports and export-oriented industries and an active search for new and diversified external markets (B. Torres, 1972: 178; Valero, 1972: 96–298). In 1970 a particularly sharp rise occurred in Mexico's current account deficit. The concentration of Mexican exports to the United States reached approximately the same soaring figure (70 percent of total exports) as in the late 1950s, after having declined somewhat in the 1960s (Pellicer de Brody, 1974: 322–323).

The first major "casualty" of the worsening economic conditions — reflected both in Mexico's international trade and in its inability to continue the sustained and rapid economic growth previously experienced — was the institutionalized concept of a "special relationship" with the United

States. Underlying this concept had been the assumption that Mexico could solve its international economic problems through bilateral agreements with its powerful northern neighbor. This approach, which was slightly modified during the 1960s, is believed to have accounted for the primary attention traditionally paid by Mexico to its bilateral contacts with the United States and its "indifference toward the diversification of its international relations" (Pellicer de Brody, 1974: 318).

At the same time that Mexico was suffering from new strains on its economic relations with other countries, there were modifications in the international system in general. The transformation of former "blocs" into multiple power centers, the rise to economic prominence of the European Economic Community and Japan, the rapprochement and reduction of tensions between the United States and the two leading Communist powers, the greater permissiveness shown by the United States toward political initiatives taken by states within its sphere of influence, and the conspicuous absence of major U.S. initiatives toward Latin America in the late 1960s led to greater freedom of action for the smaller and peripheral states. The semiofficial *Comercio Exterior* stated (March 1973: 3) that "this new world situation offers the developing countries, Mexico among them, new perspectives." Echeverría elaborated on the way changes would affect Mexico's international stance in a speech to the Congress on February 21, 1973: "The appearance of new power centers, the destruction of seemingly unshakable alliances, the relaxation of tensions and the understanding—secret at first and then manifest—between former rivals, clearly indicate that we have arrived at the end of the cold war. The shift from bipolarity to multipolarity has determined the greater participation of small and medium sized nations at international forums" (Comercio Exterior, English ed., March 1973: 3).

The Mexican government translated this evaluation into concrete action, reflected in Echeverría's first "grand tour" (March-April 1973) of Canada, Great Britain, Belgium, France, the Soviet Union, and China. A decade earlier (1963), President López Mateos, in an innovative move designed to achieve similar objectives, visited Yugoslavia and

Poland, and intensified commercial contacts with the Soviet Union. Nevertheless, López Mateos, hesitant about overly deviating from accepted practice, failed to include the Soviet Union in his 1963 trip and reacted cautiously to Soviet signals of interest in closer relations (Pellicer de Brody et al., 1973: 23). Although a Mexican trade mission visited China in 1964, it was only with the improvement of United States-Chinese relations that the Mexican government felt it could follow suit.

Echeverría's Subjective Impact on Foreign Policy

Although both economic considerations and the more relaxed conditions in the international sphere are essential to understanding changes in Mexico's international economic strategy, these constitute only a part, albeit an important one, of the complex set of factors shaping Echeverría's responses in this area of national policy. The others are rooted in the president's formative political experience, his perceptions of the ordering of governmental priorities, his interactions with various groups, and his personal style.

An arresting feature of Echeverría's thinking on Mexico's international relations is that his innovations in no way resulted from a serious policy-planning process or careful preliminary study. Several students of Mexican foreign affairs (Pellicer de Brody, 1972; Valero, 1972) agree that Echeverría's foreign policy was formulated intuitively and with little or no planning. Rather than developing along a clearly preconceived course, policy was shaped into its final "radicalized" form through a series of responses geared to redress rapidly changing internal and external circumstances.

Ample proof of Echeverría's improvisation is contained in his campaign speeches of 1969–1970. He expressed primary interest in domestic affairs, which can only be partially explained by the nature of the audiences on his nationwide tours and his lack of experience in foreign affairs. A more plausible interpretation is that in his own set of priorities, to a great extent influenced by the domestic focus of the 1968 upheaval, foreign policy took a back seat when compared to

internal issues. This was clearly reflected in the more volu-
minous, better organized, and more coherent presentation of
the domestic part of his electoral platform. Those references
to foreign policy made by the presidential candidate were
scant, devoid of innovative content, and had little bearing on
later developments. Retrospectively, they show adherence to
traditional Mexican diplomatic norms and carry no dis-
cernible new message. In some instances, the topics chosen by
Echeverría even turned out to be anachronistic in the light of
subsequent developments.

One finds a disproportionately lengthy discussion about
the need for strengthening economic and cultural ties with
Franco Spain "because many are the bonds that unite us with
that country" (Echeverría, 1971: Vol. II–III, 54–61). In
addressing the problem of the balance-of-trade deficit, Echeverría (1971: Vol. II–III, 126–127) prescribed conventional
formulas such as establishing an interministerial council to
coordinate the export drive, promoting tourism, and indus-
trializing and expanding the domestic market as a means for
achieving the goal of economic independence. Although he
mentioned (1971: Vol. II–III, 53) that producers of raw
materials face common problems, he referred to international
solidarity in specific relation to Latin America — focusing on
the need to promote regional integration — and not the more
comprehensive Third World. The need to expand relations
with regions outside the Western Hemisphere was only
vaguely alluded to (Echeverría, 1971: Vol. VI, 48–49). When
discussing the guiding principles of Mexican foreign policy,
Echeverría (1971: Vol. I, 19–50; Vol. VI, 46–47) merely
reiterated a list that included self-determination, nonintervention, the juridical equality of all nations, and the pacific
settlement of disputes, as well as Mexico's concept of a
nuclear-free Latin America.

On the whole, Echeverría's responses to questions posed
during his campaign concerning future initiatives in international relations reflected a dearth of coherent, specific plans
and targets and indicated no intention of embarking on an
activist foreign policy. For example, when asked on January
5, 1970 whether he planned any foreign tours, Echeverría

(1971: Vol. I, 49–50) replied that he would like to visit "those Latin American countries which were not visited by Presidents López Mateos and Díaz Ordaz" and those countries "with which it is necessary to increase commercial-economic exchange in general." After becoming president, he responded even more strikingly to a similar question raised during a visit by his Costa Rican colleague: Echeverría intimated that he did not intend to leave the country for the next "two or three years" (Valero, 1972: 293; Cosío Villegas, 1974: 88).

In retrospect, two fundamental characteristics of Echeverría's foreign policy seem to support the contention that its activist-"radical" nature was, to a large extent, an outgrowth of his frustrated domestic reformism: foreign policy was directed toward finding a complementary, if not an alternate, strategy for solving outstanding national problems, and it was simultaneously dedicated to increasing internal political support for the president. These two salient features reflect two distinct, though interrelated, conspicuous gaps — one chronological and the other thematic — concerning the relationship between domestic and foreign policies during his administration.

The chronological gap is that Echeverría's activism in foreign affairs began significantly later than his reform measures on the domestic front. Some (Hamilton, 1975: 54) mark 1973 as the starting point. A close look at such indicators as the number of remarks about international relations in presidential addresses, presidential trips abroad, and, to a lesser extent, new diplomatic ties, however, suggests that greater emphasis on foreign policy activism emerged in 1972, but still lagged behind important domestic initiatives and followed what appears to have been the most serious internal challenge to Echeverría's leadership during his presidency, that is, the *Halcones* affair of June 1971.

Viewed in the broader time perspective of his entire *sexenio,* the resistance encountered in promoting significant and overdue domestic reforms that might correct socioeconomic disequilibria provided the basic rationale and impetus for the search for a supplementary strategy to help alleviate national economic difficulties and prevent sacrificing the president's reformist momentum, albeit on a different front.

Improvement of Mexico's international economic position through a persistent multilateral action—organizing and uniting weak Third World producers of raw materials and importers of industrial goods and foreign technology to extract better terms from the developed industrial powers — gradually emerged as the parallel strategy that could benefit Mexico directly, as well as improve the plight of other developing states. This had one obvious advantage over the domestic redistributive thrust: it would not encounter the same intensive interest group opposition, even though it did not hold the promise of being more successful.

Thus, an inverse relationship progressively developed in which the greater the frustration with domestic reform efforts, the greater the emphasis on foreign policy initiatives. The rise of foreign policy activism and the growing coherence in its formulation (if not always in its application) were accompanied by a watered-down reformist thrust on the home front. While the first three years or so of President Echeverría's administration witnessed attempts at redistributive and nationalist economic legislation and internal political reforms, in the second half of his term these increasingly gave way to stop-gap domestic measures designed primarily to combat inflation and a concomitant shift to foreign policy activism.

The significant foreign policy initiatives that did take place during the early period of Echeverría's term were still motivated by conventional economic considerations and had no pronounced political undertones. They were also conducted by means of traditional tactics. During this phase, described as the stage of "commercial diplomacy" (Pellicer de Brody, 1972: 149), top-level meetings between Echeverría and the Central American presidents of Guatemala, Costa Rica, Nicaragua, and Honduras took place in the second half of 1971, and the president made a trip to Japan in March 1972. These contacts were aimed at securing new export markets and, in the case of Japan, at seeking technological and financial assistance in order to diversify Mexico's external, economic dependence.

The unexpected transition from an initial low-keyed "commercial diplomacy" to a much more politicized and aggressive approach was caused by a fusion of economic and political motives that grew out of developments peculiar to 1971. One external economic factor that contributed considerably to this transition (Pellicer de Brody, 1972) was the introduction in August 1971 of the 10 percent surcharge tax by the Nixon administration. After the failure of Mexico's efforts to persuade its major trading partner to waive this tax, Echeverría went to the United Nations General Assembly (October 1971). For the first time he chose to present his economic grievances in a multilateral arena, and he coupled this novelty with the equally novel appeal for Third World solidarity and public censure of the United States for economic protectionism (Secretaría de la Presidencia, 1971). Thus, the launching of the Third World (*tercermundista*) appeals and "revisionist" economic argumentation at the UN, while chronologically falling within the "commercial diplomacy" stage, already signaled the new tendency.

Domestic political considerations came to the fore at the time of Echeverría's trip to Chile in April 1972. Although his main purpose was to present Mexico's nascent Charter of States' Economic Rights and Duties — later to become the backbone of his foreign policy "philosophy" — at the third session of the United Nations Committee on Trade and Development (UNCTAD) there was another major objective. By forging close relations with Salvador Allende's socialist-and Marxist-oriented government, the Mexican president could place himself at the forefront of Latin America's progressive vanguard and draw upon it as a source of legitimation among progressives at home. His defense of Chile's right to nationalize its economic resources, his denunciation of foreign meddling in its domestic affairs, and his general support of the Allende government were attractive to those members of the domestic public he was courting most, that is, the intellectual and university communities, as well as other elements within the progressive camp. The need to convince these Mexican circles of the president's reformist and liberal sincerity and to rally their support behind him became more acute after the first round of feeble domestic economic and political measures failed to produce any immediate dramatic impact. The president's handling of the *Halcones* affair cast severe doubts within liberal-progressive groups about his incipient *Apertura* policy, while the incident and its aftermath revealed the extent of right-wing and conservative opposition to his policies. Internal economic immobilism, which plagued the first year of the *sexenio,* further accentuated the need for momentum in foreign policy. In 1971 national economic growth dropped sharply, to a mere 3.1 percent increase in gross internal product, as against an average rise of 7 percent in the 1960s (Pellicer de Brody, 1972: 150).

Additionally, President Salvador Allende's four-day visit to Mexico (late November and early December 1972) heavily contributed to the strengthening of Echeverría's position in leftist-leaning quarters. One source sees an analogy between the political service provided by Salvador Allende to Echeverría during his Mexican visit and the one rendered to Allende himself by Fidel Castro, who had visited Chile a year earlier: "Both presidents, in rather different circumstances, needed reinforcement from a renowned left-wing leader to bolster their political support and quieten a turbulent Left" (Latin America, December 8, 1972). A somewhat similar parallel can be drawn between the inflammatory impact of the visits by the two Latin American champions of Marxism and socialism on conservative and right-wing elements in Mexico and Chile. Yet, on balance, the political benefits that accrued to Echeverría seem to have outweighed this disadvantage. Through joint appearances before crowds of workers, peasants, and students, where Allende referred to the identical political aims of the two governments and praised Echeverría's leadership, the Chilean president helped Echeverría mobilize leftist support and fortify the nationalist and "radical" image he had invariably tried to project.

After Allende's visit, Echeverría continued to find relations with Chile a fruitful source of external "revolutionary legitimation."[16] When Chile's economic situation was deteriorating and external credits were scarce, Mexico, in clear defiance of the United States extended credits to Chile that reached $80 million at the time of Allende's fall. In 1973 the Mexican government rushed an emergency shipment of 400,000 barrels of fuel to Chile. Both gestures were made when Mexico itself was heavily indebted to other countries and imported considerable quantities of petroleum (Jones and Lafrance, 1976: 61). These moves aroused conservative criticism at home but were instrumental in improving the president's relations with the "progressive Left."

After Allende's regime succumbed to the military junta, Echeverría appears to have intensified domestic use of the Chilean issue. In a series of antijunta diplomatic moves, Echeverría kept the issue highly visible. The open expression of indignation and official mourning that followed the September 1973 coup and Allende's death, the granting of asylum to his widow and family, and the furnishing of safe conduct passes to political refugees by the Mexican Embassy in Santiago were only the opening gestures. The ambassador to Chile was recalled for an indefinite period, and at a later date Secretary for Foreign Affairs Emilio Rabasa was sent on a controversial, though somewhat successful, mission to secure the release of prominent ex-officials and political refugees crowding the Mexican Embassy.

On November 26, 1974, in its most drastic move yet, Mexico severed relations with the military junta. Observers analyzing the motivations behind this decision point to the salience of domestic political considerations: "At that time the Echeverría administration was in the process of imposing ... fiscal reform throughout the country and needed as much reformist backing as it could obtain. With the selection of his successor less than a year away, Echeverría was no doubt making a bid to consolidate the Left behind his effort to name a reformist candidate who would continue his policies" (Jones and Lafrance, 1976: 70). According to these authors, the Echeverría administration continued to pursue an active antijunta policy after the break; it hosted (February 1975) the third session of the International Commission Investigating Crimes of the Military Junta in Chile and publicized its positions through various other channels.

As in the case of Chile under Allende, Mexico's choice of partners on the international scene, in several conspicuous cases, was dictated by their potential for serving domestic political objectives. This was particularly true regarding Mexican identification with a select number of Latin American governments possessing appropriate characteristics. Because relations with Chile were a prime vehicle for serving internal needs, the eventual fate of the Allende government necessitated the development of adequate external substitutes to fulfill a similar internal function as nationalist-leftist legitimizers. Thus, long before the Chilean theme was exhausted as a rallying banner, and immediately following Allende's tragic and abrupt disappearance from the scene, Echeverría did not lose much time in cultivating and promoting new progressive partnerships. Given the understandable constraints limiting Echeverría's interactions with military regimes in the Western Hemisphere—due to his professed democratic-liberal commitments and *Aperturismo*—the only available possibilities were to be found with the governments of Venezuela and Cuba.

The nationalist-activist performance of Carlos Andrés Pérez in hemispheric affairs, and the social democratic character of his government at home, made the Venezuelan president a most valuable partner for his Mexican counterpart. Echeverría and Andrés Pérez found fruitful arenas for the collective expression of their nationalist, anti-imperialist postures, most concretely in the promotion of new Latin American economic-political groupings such as the Latin American Economic System (SELA) and the Caribbean Multinational Shipping venture (NAMUCAR). These organizations, formed in 1975, were based on regional membership that included Cuba but not the United States. The political sting behind these new multilateral frameworks was not concealed by Echeverría, who (1976) openly proclaimed:

This was the intention behind the Mexican proposal . . . on 15 June 1974 for the Latin American Economic System and later for the Caribbean Multinational Shipping Line. These two organizations were formally organized in October and December 1975, respectively, with the membership of twenty-five Latin American countries in the first case and with six Caribbean states in the second. The SELA and the NAMUCAR, as well as the various associations for promoting raw materials which we have begun to organize, evidence the beginning of truly Latin American economic cooperation without metropolitan inclusions or advice.

While Mexican-Venezuelan coauthorship proved the key to some advances in furthering Latin American autonomy vis-à-vis the United States, the newly developed interaction with Cuba could be used to greater symbolic effect for domestic purposes. Contacts with Cuba were intensified well beyond those undertaken by previous Mexican administrations after Castro's rise to power. The new role of Mexican-Cuban relations was signaled by Rabasa's visit to Havana of March 29 to April 1, 1974 — the first by a Mexican foreign secretary since 1959. Francisco Javier Alejo, Echeverría's economic adviser who also visited Cuba at that time, stated (April 10) that Mexico would systematically expand trade relations with Castro's regime. As early as 1973, economic relations had assumed considerable proportions, at least for the Cubans; Mexico purchased $310 million worth of Cuban goods out of the island's total foreign trade of $2.6 billion for that year (Facts on File, 1974: 423).

Mexico also increased pressure for Cuba's reentry into the inter-American system. Bilateral economic and cultural programs proliferated rapidly, and the Mexican first lady, María Esther Zuno de Echeverría, headed a Mexican cultural delegation in January 1975. The process culminated with the arrival in Havana of the president himself in August 1975. Interestingly enough, official references to Cuba soon outweighed earlier references to Venezuelan-Mexican ventures. While in Echeverría's annual address of September 1, 1974 Venezuela was mentioned seven times, Cuba was not mentioned even once (of a total of fifty-seven references to foreign countries or groupings). In his 1975 annual address, Cuba merited six references, twice as many as Venezuela (of a total of sixty-six references to foreign countries).

Upon resigning as Echeverría's secretary for foreign affairs, Emilio Rabasa enumerated the major achievements of

Mexico's foreign policy during the five-year period. He placed Mexico's efforts for the removal of sanctions against Cuba by the Organization of American States and the related decision adopted by the OAS at San José, Costa Rica (late July 1975) at a respectable fifth place. This followed immediately (in descending order) the Charter of States' Economic Rights and Duties, the establishment of a 200-mile maritime economic zone, solution of the Rio Colorado salinity controversy with the United States, and Echeverría's comprehensive meetings with heads of state. The Cuban theme even preceded such prominent nationalist-progressive issues as support of UN membership for China and the establishment of diplomatic relations with it (Secretaría de Relaciones Exteriores, October-November-December 1975).

The utilization of foreign policy themes for domestic purposes is well reflected in the content of major presidential speeches, i.e., the *Informe presidencial* presented every September 1. A rough count of the number of lines devoted to foreign policy issues by Echeverría in the six *informes* between 1971 and 1976 indicates the prominent role accorded to such appeals. References to foreign affairs comprised approximately 7 percent of the first *informe,* covering the opening nine months of the administration, which attests to the initial low interest in the subject. By the second *informe* these references had climbed to 16 percent of the total and they were stabilized at about that level for the rest of the *sexenio* (1973, 15 percent; 1974, 17 percent; 1975, 17 percent; and 1976, 18 percent).

The last *informe* is particularly instructive, as it summarized the administration's cumulative record in various policy areas and enabled the chief executive to present selectively what he considered to be the salient foreign policy initiatives and accomplishments of his government. Again, his choice of international relations themes reveals a strong emphasis on issues that evoked domestically oriented messages. Taken as a whole, references to foreign policy in the sixth *informe* were designed to project the image of a president who not only was a dynamic and principled statesman who fought imperialism vehemently, advocated the cause of exploited Third World countries, and spearheaded a comprehensive effort to reform the international system for the sake of greater world justice, but also—and no less importantly—was an untiring champion of democracy, human rights, and freedom. Among those appeals oriented toward domestic consumption, the Chilean and Spanish cases figured prominently. While both issues, particularly that of Chile, had been utilized extensively earlier in the *sexenio,* their reiteration at the closing of Echeverría's term assumed an added urgency because of domestic developments, especially in mid-1976, that helped tarnish the democratizing image of his administration.

Among these events were the presidential elections of July 4 and the *Excelsior* shuffle of July 8. In the elections of 1976, the PAN, the only contender for political power to face the PRI, did not field a candidate for the first time in thirty years. Although this primarily resulted from the *Acción Nacional's* inability to agree on a nominee, because of internal divisions (for details, see Latin America, December 5, 1975) rather than a decision to de-legitimize the PRI through abstention, the actual effect was not much different. As the two other official opposition parties, the PPS and PARM, endorsed the PRI's presidential candidate, the PAN's nonparticipation created the political vacuum dreaded by the ruling elite, leaving its candidate, José López Portillo, unopposed by any officially recognized party. The PAN's failure to nominate a candidate brought to a halt a democratic trend that had gathered force since the early fifties, that is, the constant rise in its share of the presidential vote from 7.8 in 1952 to 13.8 percent in 1970 (Segovia, 1974: 60). This trend had been essential to substantiating the elite's claim that the political party system was competitive.

Another major antidemocratic development originated at the top of the PRI hierarchy and was directed against the nation's best and most influential daily newspaper, *Excelsior.* The purge of its editor, Julio Scherer, and six staff members clearly reeked of political motives and was carefully prepared and cynically executed. *Excelsior,* which had enjoyed Echeverría's blessing until at least late 1975, had distinguished itself by maintaining an independent and critical editorial policy, thereby constituting an important manifestation of the president's *Apertura* policy. Whatever the precise motives behind the purge (for more, see Latin America, July 23, 1976), it dealt a severe blow to the government's liberalizing image.

Thus, concern for the fate of democracy abroad, as expressed in critical references to events in Spain and elsewhere, was intended to help mitigate the impact of setbacks to democracy at home. One finds in the last *informe* (Echeverría, 1976), for example: "In defense of human rights and with concern over the threat to peace, we denounced before the United Nations the serious events which took place in Spain last year. We are carefully watching the democratization process in Spain and we hope, together with the progressive sectors of this nation, that its pace will be stepped up."

Similarly, the question of establishing diplomatic relations with Spain was presented as conditional upon good democratic behavior:

When we have been asked what conditions we would require of the Spanish Government . . . what kind of a situation would be necessary to lead us to ask for resuming relations, with great modesty, I have answered . . . that we think that there should be a path that will ensure a parliament where all the political parties are represented, which will consolidate the freedom of the press, that all prisoners be released, that the emigrants — regardless of any distinction — be allowed to return home. Only in this manner will we have fulfilled our commitment to the Spanish people.

Collectively, Echeverría's reactions to internal developments in Spain and to the Chilean military junta amounted to a semblance of a diplomatic recognition policy used with much bravado to champion the cause of democracy: "Our rejection of the policy of force led us to condemn all violations of human rights and all dictatorial persecution for political reasons. In line with this attitude we broke diplomatic relations with the present Chilean regime, which ousted—with foreign support—the constitutional government of the patriotic president, Salvador Allende."

The granting of asylum, primarily to Chilean political refugees, constituted another major appeal of the last *informe* to progressive-leftist circles at home:

> This institution gains special significance at a time when the violations of individual rights are generalized in an alarming manner in the continent. I am proud to report before this sovereign assembly that throughout the present administration almost 2,000 persons of various nationalities requested and obtained protection in our embassies. We are very proud of having granted asylum to Allende's widow — that great Latin American woman who resembles so much, because of her situation and action, Margarita de Juárez — and many hundreds of Chileans who are working in our universities.

The chronological gap in the relationship between domestic and foreign policy under Echeverría was pointed out earlier. The second gap, which is implicit in the previous discussion and suggests a similar conclusion, is the thematic incongruence between "radical" foreign policy and moderate domestic reformism. This perceived "split image" of Echeverría was best expressed in a question put to him in a press conference during his August 1975 visit to Cuba: "You have insisted, sir, that your foreign policy corresponds to your domestic policy, to the extent that both are the two faces of the same political attitude; nevertheless, public opinion . . . believes that while being undeniably progressive in your foreign policy, you have not managed to be so in your domestic policy" (Comercio Exterior, September 1975: 87).

The existence of this incongruence can be explained both by the domestically oriented use of foreign policy, as well as by its decisional dynamics. The latter refers to the fact that Mexican interest groups tend to be much less involved in foreign policy making than in domestic issues, including those groups who are most active and exert the most pressure. This has resulted in wider discretion for the president in formulating and styling foreign policy initiatives and greater tolerance for radical rhetoric and appeals concerning such matters than there are in the exercise of domestic policy. Until the middle of Echeverría's term, only one conspicuous exception to this "rule" had occurred in contemporary Mexican politics: the heated involvement of interest groups in Mexico's Cuba policy between 1960 and 1961. Carlos Astiz (1974: 222), in his discussion of this episode, states: "For the first time in a number of years, a foreign policy decision became a matter of public controversy." But even then, the groups that opposed the policy cared more about its domestic implications than its substance as foreign policy.

While the customary low level of involvement in international relations facilitates presidential initiatives in that area, Echeverría's renewed and heightened use of foreign policy themes for internal elite legitimation gave foreign policy its radical and aggressive tinge. Astiz (1974), drawing on data included in the Almond and Verba cross-national study of political cultures, has pointed out that both Mexico's ruling elite and a sample of its population assigned a low priority to international politics as compared to internal goals. This suggests that previous governments had made limited use of foreign policy issues to bolster their "revolutionary" image at home. During the Echeverría administration the practice was drastically altered, at least after 1972. Consistently and intensively, foreign policy themes were utilized to present the government to the nation as vigorously change-oriented.

At the same time, activist-"radical" foreign policy considerably surpassed a more sluggish and incremental internal reformism. The fact that the president repeatedly insisted that the two were "two faces of the same political attitude" is indicative of the reinforcement effect he wished to extract from the external for the internal arena. As in the older Cuban controversy, this introduced a foreign policy issue into the agenda of grievances feeding domestic conflicts. There is little wonder that the president's Chilean policy triggered angry reactions from conservative and right-wing Mexican quarters, whom Echeverría described on various occasions as "the enemies of Mexico" and belittled as "small, improvised pressure groups." This is how he put it in the sixth *informe:* "Various publications have recently reported — among other lies by the small pressure groups which have been improvised by the furious enemies of Mexico — that important political institutions of Mexico are being directed by Chileans in asylum. This is one of the many lies which is being spread about Mexico" (Echeverría, 1976).

The Changing Patterns of Foreign Policy

As for the much-debated question of how innovative Echeverría's foreign policy actually was, the answer entails more than the assertion that it was more active and aggressive (or even revisionist) vis-à-vis the status quo than beforehand, although these two characteristics are obviously the most salient. Guy Poitras (1974: 70) has argued that the major thrust of Echeverría's foreign policy can be subsumed under its three main responses to the condition of economic dependence: the Charter of States' Economic Rights and Duties, the passing of legislation concerning foreign investment and the transfer of technology, and the expansion of Mexico's interaction with the rest of Latin America in order to bring about regional unity. William Hamilton (1975: 56) has added two novelties, Mexico's active participation in SELA and the NAMUCAR, although they might conceivably fit into Poitras's third response. A more complete evaluation of Echeverría's innovations, however, requires an examination of the continuity and change that characterize the central aspects of Mexican foreign policy, including its goals, guiding principles, arenas for interaction with other countries, instruments, style, and uses.

Although on various occasions Echeverría gave his solemn commitment to "our historical principles," referring specifically to the sovereign equality of all states, nonintervention, and self-determination, at the same time he spoke about the "generation of new concepts." The most important new feature was the adoption of a more active and dynamic international presence — the refusal to let Mexico continue to be "a passive spectator of history" (Comercio Exterior, March 1973: 4). Thus, he eschewed the traditional Mexican posture of minimal participation in international affairs, an established characteristic that had been elevated, according to one observer (Stevens, 1974: 33), "to the category of a transcendent moral principle." As noted previously, this passivity had been manifested during the 1960s by a limited interest in initiatives for Latin American economic integration and — except for the López Mateos interlude — by a largely indifferent attitude toward the development of relationships outside the Western Hemisphere.

The abandonment of the traditional strategy of stressing bilateral relations with the United States manifested itself primarily in the dramatic proliferation, under Echeverría's administration, of Mexico's interactions with other countries, regions, and economic-political groupings. This was reflected in the unprecedented expansion of the network of diplomatic representation, the conclusion of a large number of bilateral agreements, Mexico's active participation in multilateral frameworks representing developing and dependent states (UNCTAD, FAO, Third World forums, and regional arenas), and the development to an extreme of a personal diplomacy in which the president — by the intensive use of face-to-face, top-level contacts and frequent tours of foreign nations — played a predominant role.

Echeverría's own appraisal (1976) of his foreign policy, as expressed in his concluding *informe,* provides major clues as to those innovative features introduced under his leadership. The fundamental characteristic of discontinuing the dominance of bilateral relations with the United States was a transition he equated to the breaking of a siege:

We have sought to overcome the barrier of isolation and encirclement of a dangerous bilateralism which could lead us to the inertia of dependence. In six years we almost doubled our friendly contacts with the world's people. At the beginning of this administration Mexico had diplomatic links with 67 nations. We currently have relations with 129 countries.

The decision to diversify the economic and technological exchanges with more than one country also led us to promote our foreign trade and carry out an active and enterprising diplomacy. In the past six years we have visited nine European countries, four Asian countries, nine African and Middle East countries and fourteen

American countries. Mexico has been the host to more than thirty high officials, chiefs of state and government and foreign ministers.

As a result of the foreign visits we made, more than 180 international agreements were signed. Approximately one-third of them involve scientific and technological cooperation or cultural matters and the rest involve economic and trade matters.

The injection of new dynamism into Mexico's foreign policy was not solely manifested in its active participation in international forums, the expansion of the geographical scope of its interaction, and its greater interest in pursuing contacts with regional groupings, such as the Andean Pact nations and Western and Eastern European economic "blocs." Of greater significance, certainly from the viewpoint of symbolizing the president as a "radical" *tercermundista,* was the ambitious attempt to revise and reform the existing international system by proposing a new code for international conduct, suggesting a restructuring of major international organizations, and setting new "ground rules" for their operation. Such attempts had a clear common denominator, that is, reducing big power supremacy and strengthening the relative position of the weaker nations, who were considered the victims of dependency and underdevelopment. Thus, Echeverría (1976) underlined the urgent need for a structural reform of the United Nations so that it would be instrumental in creating "a new world order":

> We proposed the strengthening of the decision-making ability of the General Assembly whose functions are currently limited in comparison with the Security Council. . . . We also advocated the reduction of the subjects on which the veto can be imposed and the extension of the veto to some of the several members of the Third World in order to achieve in the Security Council a representation which corresponds to the actual current composition of the international scene.

A more successful corollary of the attempt to revamp the United Nations was the promotion of the Charter of States' Economic Rights and Duties, which purported to organize and codify a new international economic order. First presented at the third UNCTAD meeting in Santiago, Chile in April 1972 and adopted on December 6, 1974 by the UN General Assembly, the charter (for a thorough analysis, see Poitras, 1974: 66–69) undoubtedly constituted the single most important foreign policy initiative under Echeverría. It was designed to correct what the president (1976) defined as the "structure of the unjust system of world exploitation based on a colonial view of work, the stealing of natural resources, and the devaluation of the raw materials and human effort of Third World countries." This document became Mexico's major Third World appeal and — as stated by Echeverría himself — a priority objective of its foreign policy.

It should be emphasized that in addition to those concrete economic results obtained by the adoption of the charter by the United Nations — which might well have been negligible — this initiative conferred considerable substance to Mexico's diplomatic activism at both the multilateral and bilateral levels and proved to be its main vehicle for establishing a respectable presence within the Third World camp. It enabled Mexico to surge forth as an acknowledged standard-bearer for the developing nations, thus stealing the show from other Latin American countries that had preceded it in developing liaisons with extracontinental Third World and nonaligned countries. At the least, the charter was therefore instrumental in furthering Echeverría's political objectives, and it consolidated Mexican leadership claims beyond the confines of the Western Hemisphere.

The Organization of American States, which was closer to home and more distinctly identified with the paramount position of the United States, served as another major target for Echeverría's (1976) international revisionism:

Our policy to reform the structure and operation of the OAS has had the same emphasis and direction. . . . Latin America forms part of the Third World. Its struggles are identical and parallel to those carried out by other nations against colonialism and modern attempts at subjugation. Latin American countries have the historical responsibility of breaking the inertia that binds them to continental relations . . . and intensifying exchange and solidarity with the peoples of other continents who are involved in the same battle for their national assertion.

At the operational level, Mexican sponsorship and initiatives were largely responsible for some democratizing moves undertaken by the OAS, such as the introduction of the principle of "ideological pluralism" — somewhat of a foreign policy counterpart to Echeverría's domestic "Democratic Opening" — into the OAS Charter and the adoption of a simple majority vote procedure for its amendment. As noted, Mexico was the moving force behind the removal of OAS restrictions on the resumption of diplomatic relations with, to quote President Echeverría, "the sister republic of Cuba."

Nevertheless, disaffection with the OAS in its present form and the difficulty of reconstructing it, as well as the desire to strengthen its members' collective bargaining position vis-à-vis the United States and find consolation in interclient cooperation, influenced Mexico's promotion of partial alternatives, such as SELA and, within its framework, the NAMUCAR. One of the most enthusiastic supporters of SELA, Premier Fidel Castro, declared on August 18, 1975 that it was "the antithesis of the Alliance for Progress" of the OAS and "one of the great initiatives of President Echeverría" (Facts on File, 1975: 820).

As for foreign policy instruments, they presented another area for renovation. Early in the *sexenio,* Olga Pellicer de Brody (1972: 147, 154) noted that the majority of Echeverría's new ambassadorial appointments were economists who introduced a novel style into Mexican diplomacy. She felt, however, that the emergent enterprising foreign policy was not supported by appropriate structures equipped with the necessary expertise to deal successfully with assigned goals. She referred primarily to the diversification of international economic relations and thus underscored the weakness of those mechanisms, public and private, designated to gather and evaluate economic information for furthering such a policy. This problem was partially attended to by the creation of the Mexican Institute for Foreign Trade (IMCE); but active participation in international relations also required the strengthening of the Foreign Ministry (*Secretaría de Relaciones Exteriores*), which had one of the lowest budgetary allocations in Mexico's public administration.

Despite the personalist impact exerted by the president in directing, styling, and actually participating in the diplomatic process, steps were undertaken during his administration to upgrade the diplomatic service, introduce greater professionalism, and expand the ministry's infrastructure. Thus, improvement of the Mexican foreign service, from the consular to the ambassadorial level, was officially presented as a major ministerial achievement for the 1970–1975 period. Under Echeverría, regional meetings of Mexican ambassadors were held for the first time, and the Mexican Institute Matías Romero for Diplomatic Studies was founded to train foreign service cadres (Secretaría de Relaciones Exteriores, October-November-December 1975: 53).

As noted previously, the most conspicuous institutional development in the foreign service reflecting the new activist approach and much-widened horizons of Mexican foreign relations was the expansion of the network of diplomatic representation. Because the first move was undertaken in February 1972 and focused on a single country, the People's Republic of China, it should be viewed more as an isolated, political-symbolic move than as a precursor of a tendency toward diplomatic expansion. In 1973, however, the trend was set in motion by the establishment of diplomatic ties with six other nations; but the choice of countries did not suggest any detectable motive, as it juxtaposed the young Western Hemisphere nations of Barbados and Guyana with Tanzania, Romania, the German Democratic Republic, and New Zealand. This moderate rate of expansion was maintained in 1974 when the five countries with which Mexico established ties (the Bahamas, Cyprus, Malaysia, Hungary, and Bulgaria) were equally diverse. The big leap occurred in 1975 when diplomatic relations were established with thirty-three countries, and the inclination toward Third World and developing nations became quite apparent. Within that group, black African, Arab, and Asian countries predominate. This hectic expansion continued unabated in the last year of the *sexenio*. During the six-year term Mexico established ties with sixty-two countries (Echeverría, 1971–1976; Secretaría de Relaciones Exteriores, 1975; Keesing's Contemporary Archives).

The other major instrument of foreign policy, that is, presidential trips abroad, demonstrated a similar pattern of development. Notwithstanding the October 1971 visit to the UN General Assembly, Echeverría's first trips began in 1972. His economic-revisionist thinking began to assert itself at the UNCTAD meeting in Santiago, Chile. His other destinations that year included Lima, Peru, and Japan and the United States where the discussions with top officials focused on economic questions. During his week-long visit to the United States (June 14–21) Echeverría conferred with Nixon and secured concessions on the pollution of the Colorado River, but the issue of trade remained unresolved. The orientation of his 1973 trips, which followed the hardening of U.S. foreign trade policies, was clearly toward diversification of economic dependence through the promotion of relations with non-U.S. world powers, which was in keeping with his view of a "multipolar world." Consequently, visits were made to Canada, the United Kingdom, Belgium (as the seat of the EEC's headquarters), France, the USSR, and China.

In 1974, when the energy and other related crises were seriously weakening Western economies, thereby eliminating them as a viable alternative for Mexico, the diplomatic thrust had to be readjusted. Now it was directed primarily toward the Latin American subsystem (Ecuador, Peru, Argentina, Brazil, Venezuela, Costa Rica, and Jamaica), as the president attempted to enlist support for the charter and to develop regional cooperation schemes, although he also made forays to the German Federal Republic, Italy, the Vatican, Austria, and Yugoslavia. His itinerary in 1975 was the most crowded and widest in scope (fifteen nations) and almost entirely enbraced Third World and developing nations in Asia, Africa, the Middle East, and the Caribbean — appropriately, it concluded in Cuba.

It should be noted that some important mutations were made in the underlying principles of Mexican foreign policy. If one considers the classic principles enumerated by Modesto Seara Vázquez (1969), which include self-determination, nonintervention, nationalism, independence, collective security, the pacific settlement of disputes, international law, the juridical equality of all nations, and disarmament, then Echeverría — on several different occasions — chose to depart from the cardinal principles of Mexican diplomatic tradition. Mexico's Chilean policy was the first notable deflection. The adoption, immediately after the September 1973 coup, of a combative and committed diplomacy beyond the pre-Echeverría practice of refusing to establish diplomatic relations with Franco Spain, South Africa, and Rhodesia was qualitatively new and occupied a commensurate place in declaratory usage. On the Venezuelan leg of his six-nation tour of Latin America in 1974, Echeverría explained why Mexico could no longer remain indifferent to occurrences in other, in this case Latin American, countries: "transgressions against our sovereignty do not occur only within our respective frontiers. It is seen threatened whenever in a sister nation foreign intervention triumphs, when democracy is being sacrificed" (Arriola, 1974: 110).

President Echeverría did not hesitate to launch criticism, even against a host government, while on an official visit. Speaking before the Brazilian legislature during the same Latin American tour and obviously deviating from accepted diplomatic norms, Echeverría let his listeners know what he thought of political authoritarianism by delivering an unsubtle message that defended political criticism and upheld the free exchange of opinions. He even invited the legislators to build constitutional institutions (Poitras, 1974: 75).

The refusal to grant official recognition to the regime in Spain had been one of the constants of Mexican foreign policy ever since Franco's victory in the 1930s. It had always been an atypical case because of its incongruence with the principles of nonintervention and self-determination, and with the veteran (1930) nonjudgmental Estrada doctrine upheld by successive Mexican governments, although intricate legal argumentation had been developed to justify the deviation.[17]

Toward the end of his administration, Echeverría decided to go beyond the traditional nonrecognition policy vis-à-vis Franco's government and added an aggressive anti-Franco touch to his arsenal of liberal-progressive appeals. The specific event that triggered this decision was the execution of five Basque nationalist *guerrilleros* by the Spanish government in late September 1975. Echeverría's reaction was surprisingly sharp. He sent a message (for excerpts and interpretation, see Análisis Político, October 6, 1975) to the UN secretary general (that was rebuffed) that condemned not only the death sentences but also the "dictatorial regime, that since the destruction of the Republic offends the Spanish people"; consequently it urged those nations that maintained relations with "the Spanish dictatorship, imposed by Nazi-Fascism" to rectify their policy. Echeverría also requested that a special Security Council meeting be held to consider suspending Spain's membership in the international organization, and he called on UN members to sever diplomatic and other relations with Franco's government. Echeverría explained this departure from the principles of self-determination and nonintervention by Mexico's refusal to tolerate "the criminal conduct of the dictatorship." The response of the Spanish delegate to the UN was equally straightforward; he noted Echeverría's alleged links with the CIA and recalled his role in the 1968 events. On September 29, Echeverría cut all commercial and communications links with Spain (Facts on File, 1975: 732).

It is apparent that the departures from hitherto established principles were motivated primarily by domestic political considerations. Thus, the active identification with a progressive radical government or, conversely, the public censuring of authoritarian practices or of an unpopular domestic policy measure undertaken by a reactionary regime were basically designed to have an impact on the public at home.

To the list of departures from established norms and basic principles might be added the visit paid by Echeverría to Pope Paul in the Vatican in early 1974. For a Roman Catholic nation that had elevated anticlericalism to a basic tenet of its "revolutionary ideology" and had refrained from establishing diplomatic relations with the Vatican for over a century, a visit by its president to the Holy See constituted a remarkable deviation. It was unprecedented — Echeverría was the first Mexican president to call upon a pope in Rome — and clearly ran counter to liberal-revolutionary traditions and practices. Here again, the primary motive was based on domestic political considerations, for the unexpected diplomatic move was designed to pacify right-wing tensions felt either in Mexican church circles or by conservative businessmen, who had grown increasingly edgy following Echeverría's reaction to the Chilean military coup and the rising tide of urban terrorism. If this was indeed the aim of what high officials tried to play down as a mere courtesy visit, it did succeed in bringing about some conciliatory responses from Catholic and conservative circles (Latin America, February 1, 1974).

Other important foreign policy decisions, although they deviated from established principles, stemmed less from domestic political considerations because of their *tercermundista* orientation. In particular, Mexico's anti-Zionist vote in the United Nations General Assembly on November 10, 1975 and its aftermath merit special attention. To understand the vote's political rationale, it must be placed in its setting. The year 1975 was characterized by a pronounced Third World emphasis. Echeverría's "three continents trip" of July 8 to August 22, which took him to the Middle East (Kuwait, Saudi Arabia, Egypt, Israel, and Jordan), was one of its major manifestations. On August 4, in Alexandria, Egypt, Echeverría unveiled the latest version of his grand visionary scheme; he proposed a Third World economic system that would embody "all the efforts which the nonaligned countries have been making lately to protect their legitimate rights in international negotiations by using their power of collective negotiation and to explore specific prospects for economic, financial, industrial and technological cooperation" (Echeverría, 1976).

Tercermundista politicking therefore required the adoption of positions in international organizations that would demonstrate Mexico's group solidarity and would help mobilize support for its unrelenting reconstructionist initiatives. Within this context, the development of an increasingly pro-Arab Middle Eastern policy, which entailed greater declaratory support for the Palestinian cause, and the decision to let the Palestine Liberation Organization open its first Latin

66

American office in Mexico City (Comercio Exterior, September 1975: 56) were geared to enlist Arab support in Third World gatherings. A precursor of the November General Assembly vote was the resolution containing a condemnation of Zionism that was adopted at the International Women's Year Conference hosted by Mexico in the summer of 1975. Mexico's anti-Zionist vote at the UN epitomized its new solidarity[18] and represented in a nutshell some intrinsic problems arising from Echeverría's conduct of foreign affairs. The vote turned out to be more costly for the Mexican government (and business) than anticipated and its repercussions far-reaching. The act itself was generally consonant with the president's professed Third World leanings (although a significant number of Third World nations refused to go along with the resolution's equation of Zionism with racism and decided to abstain), but at the same time, it accentuated his abandonment of the traditional principles of nonintervention and self-determination, as well as departed from Mexico's previous noninvolvement in and largely equidistant position on the Arab-Israeli conflict. Furthermore, it set in motion a sequence of events that exemplified the limits imposed on Mexico's foreign policy by its economic vulnerability and dependence on the United States. The affair culminated in the resignation of Secretary for Foreign Affairs Rabasa and served as a major catalyst for the reorganization of Mexico's Foreign Ministry.

The Mexican vote was met by strong indignation not only in Israel, whose existential-ideological underpinnings are based on the message contained in Zionism as the Jews' national liberation movement, but also within the American Jewish community. The U.S. Jewish community swiftly demonstrated its solidarity with Israel by urging a tourist boycott of Mexico. According to the president of the Mexican hotel association, cancellations of hotel reservations by American Jews and their sympathizers soared within a week to 30,000. The 25 percent drop in tourism — Mexico's second largest foreign currency earner — suffered during the winter holiday season of 1975 was attributed mainly to the American Jewish boycott (Jerusalem Post, December 31, 1975). Consequently, former President Miguel Alemán, himself a major tourist industry figure and head of the Mexican tourist office in the United States, was instructed to confer with Jewish leaders in New York and invite them to meet with Echeverría in Mexico.

In early December, Echeverría sent Emilio Rabasa to Jerusalem to try to resolve the triangular conflict involving Mexico, Israel, and the U.S. Jewish community. Rabasa stayed for a week and did his best to placate the Israelis. He laid a wreath on the tomb of Theodor Herzl, the founder of modern political Zionism, and poignantly declared at a dinner in his honor given by Foreign Minister Yigal Allon: "In Zion there is no discrimination at all. . . . There is absolute tolerance. And where there is no discrimination—there cannot exist a racist people" (Jerusalem Post, December 8, 1975).

Rabasa's performance during his visit to Israel, while it seemed to have placated the Israelis, produced precisely the opposite effect on Mexican public opinion. His actions and declarations, which openly contradicted the November UN vote and followed pressure exerted by U.S. Jewish organizations, were interpreted by the Mexican press as a major humiliation. Even President Echeverría, who just a few days earlier had assured fifteen U.S. and Canadian Jewish leaders he had invited to Mexico that his country did not identify Zionism with racism (Ha'aretz, December 14, 1975), stated at the closing ceremony of the 1975 sessions of the Congress that "any Mexican would prefer to die before apologizing and, first of all, the President of the republic" (Jerusalem Post, January 1, 1976). Excelsior, articulating a generally held feeling, insisted that the guidelines of Mexico's foreign policy should be "neither improvised nor respondent to pressures, but neither should they be impolitic or injurious to the values of Mexican diplomatic tradition" (Latin America, December 19, 1975). To save face, some dramatic action had to be undertaken; under the circumstances, the secretary's presentation of his resignation on December 29, 1975 was almost inevitable. Never sufficiently explained to the public, the resignation gave rise to various speculations concerning the president and Rabasa's role in the affair (see *Análisis Político,* January 5, 1976).

In 1975, Mexico also significantly changed its stand on the conflict between Great Britain and Guatemala over the future of Belize (British Honduras). Earlier that year, Echeverría implied that Mexico had shelved its conditional claims on the northern section of Belize, which seemed to be a move toward greater support of the Guatemalan territorial demands (*Latin America,* November 14, 1975). Then, Echeverría concluded a three-day visit to Guatemala in November 1975, at a time of escalating tensions between Guatemala and Great Britain over the territory, with an unexpected statement signifying a basic shift in Mexico's position. He declared that Mexico, too, had rights to Belizean territory which could be reactivated. This visit was followed by trips by Rabasa to Belize and the UN headquarters (November 1975), where he reiterated Mexico's rights and interests in Belize and withdrew a settlement proposal (conciliatory to Guatemala) previously submitted by his government to the UN. The move was seen by some observers (*Análisis Político,* November 24, 1975) as a counterbalance to the Guatemalan claims and thus an endorsement of Belize's aspirations for independence. The transition from a pro-Guatemalan to a pro-Belizean stand can be viewed as an adoption by Mexico of a position more in line with that of the Third World and a growing number of Caribbean nations. Belize's aspirations for independence had received strong support from English-speaking nations in the Caribbean, as well as from Cuba and the nonaligned nations, who vocalized it during their meeting in Lima in August 1975. Venezuela even preceded Mexico in adopting a pro-Belizean stance (see *Latin America,* November 14, 1975).

The changing patterns of Mexico's foreign policy under President Echeverría placed an ever-growing strain on its traditional guiding principles. It became increasingly clear that a committed, more politicized, and activist foreign policy could not easily coexist with those older cardinal principles reflecting a defensive, legalistic, and largely nonpartisan orientation. Echeverría's expression of allegiance to "our historical principles" did not reconcile this built-in conflict, and the number of "special cases" or deviant foreign policy decisions and diplomatic initiatives was constantly on the rise. Political considerations, which arose from either a *tercermundista* orientation or the need to invoke liberal-democratic appeals for domestic consumption, outweighed older foreign policy principles in the formulation of several important decisions. Thus, Third World politicking was largely responsible for Mexico's UN vote on Zionism and for the modification of its stand on Belize. Echeverría's Chilean and Spanish policies, on the other hand, were salient examples of decisions geared toward domestic political purposes. The Vatican visit was another notable addition to the growing list of incongruencies or departures from traditional concepts and practices.

This process, which culminated in the UN anti-Zionist blunder, is believed to have prompted Echeverría's final significant reform in the institutional setting of the foreign policy-making process, introduced at the beginning of his last year in office. One of the first acts of Alfonso García Robles, who replaced Emilio Rabasa as secretary for foreign affairs, was to announce the establishment of a new division in his ministry entrusted with special international studies (*Subsecretaría de Asuntos y Estudios Internacionales Especiales*). Jorge Castañeda, an experienced diplomat and international relations theorist, was designated as its chief. A major task of this new division is to try to forge greater coherence between foreign policy decisions and traditional diplomatic postulates (for more, see Análisis Político, January 19, 1976). This step may well prove instrumental in avoiding the kind of embarrassing situation that led to Rabasa's resignation and in providing the president with an institutional aid for arriving at more prudently considered decisions.

V.   CONCLUSION

A ny study of contemporary Mexican politics would mark the year 1968 as a point of departure that opened a new chapter in the nation's modern history. The importance of the 1968 events, the most acute domestic political crisis in the postrevolutionary period, becomes even more apparent when the Echeverría era is examined.

During the crisis of 1968, Mexico's dissident university community functioned as a semipolitical party. Through its representative body, the National Strike Committee, it autonomously developed pressure tactics and demands on a scale and intensity never before experienced in Mexico. In the short run, these were rejected as illegitimate by the government and drew an immediate punitive reaction. In the long run, however, the protest exercised a detectable influence on government policies and constituted the major systemic stimulant for the reformism of President Luis Echeverría.

Such an impact highlights the political importance of an activist university community for effecting societal changes by directly challenging the ruling elite. The democratizing role played by the university community assumes particular significance in an authoritarian regime that professes democratic, participatory principles while actually conceding little autonomy to political structures representing lower-class interests.

This lack of sanctioned autonomy, in turn, was a major factor in the emergence of the noncaptive university community as a substitute interest aggregation structure. For this reason, the 1968 protest represents a sui generis phenomenon with thematic and functional characteristics that clearly distinguish it from Mexican nonuniversity protest "movements" of the late 1950s and early 1960s.

Although to a large extent they stemmed from stimuli generated directly by the university community's actions and criticisms during the 1968 confrontation, the president's reform efforts were never far-reaching enough to reestablish confidence between him and the nation's progressive Left. Simultaneously, his domestic initiatives were perceived as sufficiently threatening to several powerful interest groups — either in the private sector's industrial and business communities and among their allies in the PRI's conservative wing, or within the well-entrenched syndicalist leadership — as to trigger an active and effective opposition. These difficulties, which were already encountered during the early stage of Echeverría's presidency, caused a considerable shift of governmental attention to a less conflict-prone arena that seemed to offer an alternate means for solving a narrower range of pressing domestic, primarily economic, problems. Hence, an increasingly retarded domestic redistributive and democratizing thrust was gradually supplemented, if not replaced, by an effort to develop a redistributive foreign policy, the tenets of which were clearly expressed in Echeverría's "manifesto," the Charter of States' Economic Rights and Duties. Thus, Mexico under Echeverría provides a prominent case of domestic sources affecting the attitude, dynamics, and political choices of the chief executive as the pivotal level and unit of foreign policy making. Internal variables were no less crucial than international stimuli in accounting for major changes in the content, style, and overall orientation of Mexico's international relations in the 1970–1976 period.

In the realm of foreign policy, President Echeverría demonstrated his remarkable ability to adapt to changing political exigencies and circumstances. His second political transformation—that is, from domestic reformer to foreign policy innovator—was no less dramatic, swift, and surprising than his first—from repressive *secretario de gobernación* to progressive, democratizing president. Thus, with no previous diplomatic experience or involvement and, as some commentators (Cosío Villegas, 1974: 87–111) openly argue, little understanding of the international political process, Echeverría soon emerged as the prominent innovator of his country's foreign affairs.

A major feature of Echeverría's foreign policy was the much-intensified utilization of international relations themes as a major source for internal revolutionary legitimation. This, in turn, influenced the choice of external issue-areas and allies to support the projected radical-progressive image of the president. Turning Mexico into an active participant in international forums and adopting a politically committed foreign policy inevitably led to a departure from several established guiding principles of Mexican diplomacy, notably those of nonintervention and self-determination. The major innovations, however, embraced more than the development of new foreign policy appeals and the abandonment of traditional principles. Other important new facets related to the selection of new arenas for activism, as well as the development or significant expansion of foreign policy instruments. The widening of the scope of Mexico's ambitions to international leadership also affected the ultimate goals of its foreign policy.

Much of this revisionist activism was economically motivated. Economic initiatives were presented primarily at multilateral forums such as the UN General Assembly, the UNCTAD, FAO, and Third World gatherings. Still other initiatives promoted in multilateral arenas were aimed at curbing big power supremacy and concomitantly strengthening the relative weight of the weaker and dependent states. These included Mexico's policies concerning the OAS and SELA at the regional level, and the United Nations, for which Mexico proposed a political restructuring, at the global level.

As indicated above, a distinct category of salient diplomatic moves was not aimed at attaining economic objectives as much as it was destined to mobilize the domestic backing of progressive, leftist circles behind the chief executive, who operated during most of his term from a narrow base of political support. This last tactic was brought to bear primarily at the bilateral, and sometimes even unilateral, levels and characterized Echeverría's policies toward Chile, Franco Spain, and, to some extent, Cuba. In relation to these countries his "radical" and aggressive style was the most pronounced. The domestically projected image of a democratizing, nationalist president was to draw support from Mexico's assumption of the external role of leadership within the nationalist, progressive, activist vanguard of Latin America. This external role required the constant cultivation of suitable hemispheric partnerships. Thus, when developments in Chile precluded its playing a supportive role, Mexico's pro-Allende policy was rapidly supplanted by the development of stronger ties with Venezuela and Cuba.

This distinction between the various subcategories of the new elements introduced by Echeverría into Mexico's foreign affairs also facilitates answering an important question: namely, what part of his policies is reversible and what has been transmitted to his successor as a longer-lasting heritage? Generally speaking, it would seem safe to contend that for the most part Echeverría's innovations are bound to endure. These include the institutional improvements in the foreign service, an expanded diplomatic network, and the intensified interaction with extracontinental regions. Among the newly developed contacts, liaison and identification with Third World nations are most likely to persist. This type of group solidarity is not only gaining a greater foothold among Latin American nations but also may provide through concerted multilateral action a long-range bargaining leverage in these countries' relations with the developed and industrial powers. The North-South controversy makes it possible to develop and promote revisionist appeals and diplomatic activity related to Mexico's national development and economic growth needs. It concerns issues that have already united a large sector of the international community behind a broadly shared consensus. Thus, problems of underdevelopment and economic dependence, long considered a major handicap or limitation imposed on the execution of an effective and autonomous foreign policy, have been astutely converted into a diplomatic resource. The activation of complaints about the injustice of the world economic order has put the industrial powers on the defensive diplomatically and, it is hoped, will force them into making concrete concessions in the longer run.

On a larger scale, *Tercermundismo* was a belated development in the evolution of Echeverría's foreign policy, which underwent various phases before reaching its final destination. Until Echeverría's rise to power, Mexico's successive

PRI governments had not perceived economic dependence on the United States as a problem. On the contrary, this dependence, which seemed to be an outcome of geopolitical determinism, was even couched in positive terms as a "special relationship" that could, and actually did, benefit Mexico economically. As a result of the change in national economic realities of the late 1960s and the diminishing effectiveness — at least temporarily — of the "special relationship" approach, dependence loomed increasingly as an issue that had to be rectified. Thus, the earliest stage of Echeverría's foreign policy witnessed the shelving of the special relationship policy toward the United States. The initial response to the issue of dependence was based on the conventional prescription to diversify foreign trade. Efforts were made to develop export markets outside the United States, primarily in the developed and industrial nations of Western Europe, Japan, and Canada, as well as in the Soviet Union and China. These efforts coincided, however, with a worsening in international economic conditions. When results therefore fell short of expectations, the focus shifted to the Latin American scene, where Mexico tried to activate and assume leadership of interclient cooperation. Only in the last phase of Echeverría's term, when it became clear that development of the Latin American option could not produce quick economic results, was a global Third World-oriented effort put into full motion. The broad Third World appeals and the call for a new world economic order reflected increasingly "messianic" thinking and a further drift from the immediate problem-solving approach that had characterized the earlier trade diversification drive.

Mexico's emergence as a champion of the Third World, while primarily instrumental in substantiating its claim to leadership in that comprehensive forum, simultaneously bolstered its bid for regional, that is, Latin American, stature. There is little evidence, however, that this policy produced tangible economic results, or that it gave Mexico any leverage in its relations with the United States. In retrospect, the expanded diplomatic interaction and the greater involvement in foreign affairs that were the corollary of an active *tercermundista* policy created an appearance of greater maneuverability in international relations and added peripheral areas where national self-assertion could be exercised, but it hardly affected either of the twin core-issues facing Echeverría, i.e., external dependence and the problem of a bogged-down domestic reformism.

Nevertheless, the primarily development-oriented goals targeted for its foreign policy are consonant with Mexico's traditional nonideological, nonmilitary, and essentially non-territorial objectives. Selecting foreign policy alternatives along these lines is also far less risky than would be a significant intensification of interaction with the socialist camp nations, given the continued dominance of bilateral relations with the United States and Mexico's dependence upon it in the crucial areas of foreign trade, aid, investment, and the acquisition of modern technologies. Mexico has consistently shunned involvement in global power struggles, and even during the heyday of Echeverría's "radical" foreign policy mutations and drive for greater autonomy in world affairs it maintained considerable prudence in its relations with the neighboring superpower. This caution was manifested in various important aspects of Mexico's international conduct, from the mild and mostly indirect criticism of the United States through reluctance to join the Organization of Petroleum Exporting Countries (OPEC), which skillfully delineated the more secure perimeters for dissent and the demonstration of foreign policy autonomy without seriously jeopardizing vital national interests.

The part of Echeverría's innovative legacy that is most likely to disappear is that which was more specifically tied to his political needs and particular political evolution. Thus, the "radical" and aggressive style that was so essential for Echeverría's image-building campaign may be deemed un-necessary by his successor, who is free from implication in the 1968 events. Furthermore, elimination of this component can serve to mend relations with the private sector, which were strained by Echeverría's domestic and external overtures to the Left. Incumbent President José López Portillo offered proof of this soon after assuming power: he had few qualms about nominating former President Gustavo Díaz Ordaz as

Mexico's first ambassador to post-Franco Spain. The come-
back to the public scene of an arch-conservative so closely
identified with government repression in the 1968 crisis would
have been absolutely unthinkable during the Echeverría
administration.

Finally, freeing Mexico's foreign policy of the more per-
sonalistic legacy left by Luis Echeverría is also bound to
significantly reduce, and possibly eliminate, the friction
developed during his presidency between new practices and
older diplomatic principles.

NOTES

1. On these foreign policy characteristics of developing nations in general, see O'Leary, 1969: 328.

2. It includes, among others: Pellicer de Brody, 1972, 1973, 1974; Valero, 1972; B. Torres, 1972; Astiz, 1974; Poitras, 1974; Arriola, 1974; Couturier, 1975; Kaye, 1975; Hamilton, 1975; Jones and Lafrance, 1976; and the entire issue of *Foro Internacional* 56 (April-June), 1974.

3. On the influence of former leaders of the MLN on the students' National Strike Committee during 1968, see Agee, 1975.

4. The term *university community* is used here instead of *university students,* traditionally the reference group for dealing with university-related political activism. University community denotes the more inclusive aggregate constituted by university-based or -affiliated interacting groups. Our aggregate therefore includes members of the teaching staff and *preparatoria* (university-affiliated preparatory schools roughly equivalent to the senior high school level in the United States) students.

5. Although fully adopted by the CNH, the "six-points" list appeared in its final form several days before the formation of that student organ on August 8. Its final version was issued by various ad hoc student and teachers' committees on August 4, 7, and 8. See documents in Ramón Ramírez, 1969: 37–39, 54–55, 59–61.

6. Nevertheless, even in 1968 there were some exceptions. Two weeklies had taken a more independent and critical stance. These are the sensational *Por Qué?* (its editor, Mario Menéndez Rodríguez, was flown to Cuba in late 1971 as part of an exchange for the rector of the Guerrero State University, who was kidnapped by guerrillas) and *Siempre,* the organ of the non-Communist Left.

7. The student movement of 1968 demonstrated its autonomy from the outset by dissociating itself from captive student organizations, primarily the progovernment FNET (*Federación Nacional de Estudiantes Técnicos*), which it accused of "treason" (Revista de la Universidad de México, September 1, 1968: 8, 10, 17).

8. For allusions to unspecified "foreign infiltration" of the movement, see Lázaro Cárdenas's letter in *El Día,* October 6, 1968. On the "non-Mexican" character of student politics, see Blanco Moheno, 1969: 236–238.

9. On the cynical attitude of those summoned to participate in the ceremony, see Jorge Carrión et al., 1969: 100.

10. For a firsthand account of the role of students and young university lecturers in the guerrilla movement, see the confessions of two teachers at the Universidad Autónoma de Nuevo León who were detained and interrogated by the police (Tribuna de Monterrey, January 19, 1972). Press references to

78

the students' prominent role in the new guerrilla activities are numerous. See also Castillo, 1971; Alvarado, 1972; and *Excelsior,* February 22, 1972.

11. The case of former CNH member, Sócrates Amado Campos Lemus, who since October 2, 1968 had spent two years and nine months in prison, is significant. Later he became an outspoken supporter of Echeverría and was nominated as coordinator for the Plan Huicot. See "Al que Madruga Dios lo Ayuda," *Siempre,* May 24, 1972.

12. Worth mentioning in this connection is the interesting statement in Reyes Heroles's inaugural address: *"queremos hombres libres en los sindicatos"* ("we want free people in the unions") (Tiempo, February 28, 1972: 11).

13. For the latest fiscal reform by then Finance Minister J. López Portillo before the Chamber of Deputies, see *Siempre,* November 13, 1974: 57–59.

14. The inadequacy of the PRI-controlled CNOP in channeling middle-class demands and grievances is a point repeatedly made by López Cámara, 1971.

15. For some critical views of the degree of Echeverría's reformism, see Pereyra, 1974: 52–65; "Cambio o no cambio en el sistema político mexicano," *Análisis Político,* April 29, 1974; Maza, 1972; and Cosío Villegas, 1974.

16. For a detailed discussion of Echeverría's Chilean policy, see Jones and Lafrance, 1976.

17. On the historical roots of Mexico's Spanish policy and exposition of the Estrada doctrine, see Seara Vázquez, 1969: 61-66, 107.

18. The Latin American vote breakdown clearly suggests Mexico's decision to identify with extracontinental Third World, Arab, and Communist countries, rather than join the majority Latin American vote. The only Latin American countries that voted for the resolution were Cuba, Guyana, Grenada, Mexico, and Brazil. Ten voted against it (the Bahamas, Barbados, Colombia, the Dominican Republic, El Salvador, Haiti, Honduras, Nicaragua, Panama, and Uruguay). Surinam was absent and the rest abstained.

BIBLIOGRAPHY

Books and Articles

AGEE, P. (1975) Inside the Company: CIA Diary. Bungay, England: Penguin Books.

ALMOND, G. A. and B. POWELL, Jr. (1966) Comparative Politics, A Developmental Approach. Boston and Toronto: Little, Brown.

——— and S. VERBA (1963) The Civil Culture: Political Attitudes and Democracy in Five Nations. Princeton: Princeton University Press.

ALVARADO, J. (1972) "El Ejemplo de los Mayores." Siempre, February 2.

ARRIOLA, C. (1974) "El Presidente Echeverría en Latinoamérica." Foro Internacional 57 (July-September): 103–115.

ASTIZ, C. A. (1974) "Mexico's Foreign Policy: Disguised Dependency." Current History 66 (May): 220–225.

BARROS SIERRA, J. (1972) Conversaciones con Gastón García Cantú. Mexico City: Siglo Veintiuno Editores.

BLANCO MOHENO, R. (1969) Tlatelolco, Historia de una Infamia. Mexico City: Editorial Diana.

BRANDENBURG, F. (1964) The Making of Modern Mexico. Englewood Cliffs, N.J.: Prentice-Hall.

BURNETT, B. G. and K. F. JOHNSON (1968) Political Forces in Latin America, Dimensions of the Quest for Stability. Belmont, California: Wadsworth Publishing.

CARRION, J., S. ARGUEDAS, D. CAZES, and F. CARMONA (1969) Tres Culturas En Agonía. Mexico City: Editorial Nuestro Tiempo.

CASTILLO, H. (1973) Libertad Bajo Protesta. Mexico City: Federación Editorial Mexicana.

——— (1971) Article in Siempre, October 13.

COSIO VILLEGAS, D. (1974) El Estilo Personal de Gobernar. Mexico: Cuadernos de Joaquín Mortiz.

——— (1973) El Sistema Político Mexicano. Third ed. Mexico: Cuadernos de Joaquín Mortiz.

——— (1972) "Los de Dentro y Los de Fuera." Excelsior, August.

COUTURIER, E. B. (1975) "Mexico," pp. 117–135 in H. E. Davis and L. C. Wilson (eds.) Latin American Foreign Policies. Baltimore and London: Johns Hopkins University Press.

FAGEN, P.R. and W.A. CORNELIUS, Jr. [eds.] (1970) Political Power in Latin America, Seven Confrontations. Englewood Cliffs, N.J.: Prentice-Hall.

80

FLORES OLEA, V. (1972) "México Un Desafío Al Sistema." Siempre, March 15.
FRIED, R. C. (1966) Comparative Political Institutions. New York: Macmillan.
GARCIA CANTU, G. (1973a) Universidad y Antiuniversidad. Mexico: Cuadernos de Joaquín Mortiz.
_____ (1973b) "La Derecha Exige Otra Matanza." Por Qué? 275, October 4.
GARIBAY, R. (1973) "Duelo y Dolo de un Abogado Patronal." Excelsior, September 20.
_____ (1971) "Máxima Energía Señor Presidente?" Excelsior, August 26.
GONZALEZ DE ALBA, L.N. (1971) Los Días y Los Años. Sixth ed. Mexico City: Ediciones Era.
GOOD, R. C. (1962) "State-Building as a Determinant of Foreign Policy in the New States," in L.W. Martin (ed.) Neutralism and Nonalignment. New York: Frederick A. Praeger.
GOODSELL, J.N. (1969) "Mexico: Why the Students Rioted." Current History 329 (January): 31–53.
HAMILTON, W. H. (1975) "Mexico's 'New' Foreign Policy: A Reexamination." Inter-American Economic Affairs 29 (Winter): 51–58.
HANSEN, R. D. (1971) The Politics of Mexican Development. Baltimore and London: The Johns Hopkins University Press.
JACOBSON, P. (1975) "Opposition and Political Reform in Mexico." The New Scholar 5: 19–30.
JOHNSON, K. F. (1971) Mexican Democracy: A Critical View. Boston: Allyn and Bacon, Inc.
JONES, E. D. and D. LAFRANCE (1976) "Mexico's Foreign Affairs under President Echeverría: The Special Case of Chile." Inter-American Economic Affairs 30 (Summer): 45–78.
KAYE, H. J. (1975) "How 'New' is Mexico's Foreign Policy." Inter-American Economic Affairs 28 (Spring): 87–92.
KAHL, J. A. (1968) The Measurement of Modernism. Austin: The University of Texas Press.
KOPLIN, R. E. (1968) "A Model of Student Politicization in the Developing Nations." Comparative Political Studies 3 (October).
LENKERSDORF, K. (1969) "The Philosophy of the 1968 Mexican Student Movement." Specialia 1: 34–42. Latin American Institute, Southern Illinois University.
LIEBMAN, A. (1971) "Student Activism in Mexico." The Annals of the Academy of Political and Social Science 395 (May): 159–170.
_____ , K.N. WALKER, and M. GLAZER (1972) Latin American University Students: A Six Nation Study. Cambridge, Mass.: Harvard University Press.
LOPEZ CAMARA, F. (1971) El Desafío de la Clase Media. Mexico: Cuadernos de Joaquín Mortiz.
LOPEZ PORTILLO, A.G. (1968) article in El Universal, August 3.

81

MADRAZZO, J. (1975) "Agita a la Política Mexicana la Fractura del Tradicional Método del Tapadismo." La Opinión (Buenos Aires), April 17.
MARTINEZ DE LA VEGA, F. (1971) "Más Rivales Cómodos Para El PRI?" Siempre, November 24.
MAZA, E. (1973) "Lo que se Juega en la Universidad." Excelsior, January 3.
_____ (1972) "Jueves de Corpus y 10 de Junio, Hipótesis sobre el Silencio." Excelsior, June 14.
MEDINA VALDES, G. (1972) Operación 10 de Junio. Mexico: Ediciones Universo.
MONSIVAIS, C. (1971) Días de Guardar. Fourth ed. Mexico City: Ediciones Era.
MORENO SANCHEZ, M. (1971) Crisis Política de México. Mexico City: Editorial Extemporáneos.
O'LEARY, M. (1969) "Linkages Between Domestic and International Politics in Underdeveloped Nations," pp. 324–346 in J.N. Rosenau (ed.) Linkage Politics. New York: The Free Press.
PAZ, O. (1972) The Other Mexico: Critique of the Pyramid. New York: Grove Press.
_____ (1970) Posdata. Mexico City: Siglo Veintiuno Editores.
PELLICER DE BRODY, O. (1974) "Mexico in the 1970s and its Relations with the United States," pp. 314–333 in J. Cotler and R. R. Fagen (eds.) Latin America and the United States: The Changing Political Realities. Stanford: Stanford University Press.
_____ (1972) "Cambios Recientes de la Política Exterior Mexicana." Foro Internacional 50 (October-December): 139–154.
_____, M. OJEDA GOMEZ, C. ARRIOLA, R. SEGOVIA, B. TORRES, and H. GARZA ELIZONDO (1973) "Documentos y Comentarios en Torno al Viaje del Presidente Echeverría (Marzo-Abril de 1973)." Foro Internacional 53 (July-September).
PEREYRA, C. (1974) "México: Los Límites del Reformismo." Cuadernos Políticos 1 (September): 52–65.
POITRAS, G. E. (1974) "Mexico's 'New' Foreign Policy." Inter-American Economic Affairs 28 (Winter): 59–77.
PONIATOWSKA, E. (1971) La Noche de Tlatelolco. Mexico City: Biblioteca Era.
PRIETO, R. (1968) "Contra Díaz Ordaz y Contra Cuba." El Día, August 7.
RAMIREZ, R. (1969) El Movimiento Estudiantil de México, Julio-Diciembre de 1968. Two vols. Mexico City: Ediciones Era.
RIDING, A. (1973a) article in Miami Herald, June 3.
_____ (1973b) "Unemployment Woes Rise in Mexico." Miami Herald, May 6.
ROSENAU, J. N. (1967) "Foreign Policy as an Issue-Area," pp. 11–50 in J. N. Rosenau (ed.) Domestic Sources of Foreign Policy. New York: The Free Press.

82

_____ (1966) "Pre-theories and Theories of Foreign Policy," pp. 27–92 in R. B. Farrell (ed.) Approaches to Comparative and International Politics. Evanston: Northwestern University Press.

SCHMITT, K. M. (1965) Communism in Mexico. Austin: University of Texas Press.

SCHMITTER, P. C. (1971) Interest Conflict and Political Change in Brazil. Stanford: Stanford University Press.

SCOTT, R. (1968) "Student Political Activism in Latin America." Daedalus 97, 1: 70–98.

_____ (1965) "Mexico: The Established Revolution," pp. 330–395 in L. Pye and S. Verba (eds.) Political Culture and Political Development. Princeton: Princeton University Press.

SEARA VAZQUEZ, M. (1969) La Política Exterior de México. Mexico City: Editorial Esfinge.

SEGOVIA, R. (1974) "La Reforma Política: El Ejecutivo Federal, el PRI y Las Elecciones de 1973." La Vida Política en México 1970–1973. Mexico: Centro de Estudios Internacionales El Colegio de México.

SHAPIRA, Y. (1977) "Mexico: The Impact of the 1968 Student Protest on Echeverría's Reformism." Journal of Inter-American Studies and World Affairs 19 (November): 557–580.

_____ (1974) "Student-Government Confrontation: Interpreting the Mexican Crisis of 1968." Scripta Hierosolymitana 26: 120–132.

SILVERT, K. H. (1964) "The University Student," pp. 222–224 in J.J. Johnson (ed.) Continuity and Change in Latin America. Stanford: Stanford University Press.

STEVENS, E. P. (1974a) "Protest Movement in an Authoritarian Regime, the Mexican Case." Comparative Politics 7 (April): 361–382.

_____ (1974b) Protest and Response in Mexico. Cambridge, Mass.: Massachusetts Institute of Technology Press.

SUCHLICKI, J. (1972) "Sources of Student Violence in Latin America — An Analysis of the Literature." Latin American Research Review 7 (Fall): 31–46.

THOMAS, D. B. and R. B. CRAIG (1973) "Student Dissent in Latin America: Toward a Comparative Analysis." Latin American Research Review 8 (Spring): 76.

TORRES, B. (1972) "México en la Estructura del Comercio y la Cooperación Internacional de los Países Socialistas." Foro Internacional 50 (October-December): 178–204.

TORRES, M. P. (1972) "Cronología del Conflicto." Revista de Revistas, December 20.

TUOHY, W. S. and B. AMES (1969–1970) Mexican University Students in Politics: Rebels without Allies? Denver: The University of Denver.

United States Committee for Justice to Latin American Political Prisoners (no date) Mexico 1968: The Students Speak. New York.

VALERO, R. (1972) "La Política Exterior en la Coyuntura Actual de México." Foro Internacional 50 (October-December): 292–310.

83

Official Documents

ECHEVERRIA ALVAREZ, L. (1976) Informe Presidencial. Washington, D.C.: Foreign Broadcast Information Service, Latin America Daily Report 6 (September 3 and 7).
———— (1975a) "Quinto Informe Presidencial." Comercio Exterior 25 (No. 9). Mexico City: Banco Nacional de Comercio Exterior, S.A.
———— (1975b) Informe de Gobierno 1974. Mexico City: Secretaría de la Presidencia, Dirección General de Documentación e Informe Presidencial.
———— (1974) Informes de Gobierno 1971–73. Mexico City: Secretaría de la Presidencia, Dirección General de Documentación e Informe Presidencial.
———— (1971) Praxis Política. Mexico City: Cultura y Ciencia Política, A.C.
Office of the President (1972–1976) Mexican Newsletter. Mexico City.
Presidencia de la República (1970–1976) El Gobierno Mexicano. Mexico City.
Secretaría de la Presidencia (1971) México en las Naciones Unidas. Mexico City: Cuadernos de Documentación, Serie Estudios 12.
Secretaría de Recursos Hidráulicos (1973) Plan Nacional Hidráulico. Presentación. Mexico City.
Secretaría de Relaciones Exteriores (1975) México de Hoy (October-November-December). Mexico City.

Periodicals

Mexican

Análisis Político (1974–1976) (Instituto Mexicano de Estudios Políticos)
Comercio Exterior (1971–1976) (Banco Nacional de Comercio Exterior, S.A.)
El Día (1968–1976)
Excelsior (1968–1976)
Foro Internacional (1971–1976)
El Heraldo de México (1968–1976)
Novedades (1968–1976)
Oposición (1972–1973) (Communist biweekly)
Por Qué? (1968–1973) (proguerrilla weekly)
Punto Crítico (1972–1973) (radical student monthly)
Revista de la Universidad de México (1968)
Revista de Revistas (1972–1973)
Siempre (1968–1976)

Sucesos (1972–1973)
Tiempo (1972)
Tribuna de Monterrey (January 19, 1972)

Non-Mexican

Facts on File (1971–1976)
Ha'aretz (1975)
Jerusalem Post (1975)
Journal of Commerce (1973)
Keesing's Contemporary Archives (1970–1976)
Latin America (1971–1976)
Miami Herald
New York Times (1968–1976)
Washington Post (1971)